A Biblical Approach to Parenting
Norman D. Stolpe

WHO'S IN CHARGE?

CRC Publications
Grand Rapids, Michigan

The Scripture quotations in this publication are from the HOLY BIBLE, NEW INTERNATIONAL VERSION, copyright 1973, 1978, 1984, International Bible Society. Used by permission of Zondervan Bible Publishers.

Who's in Charge?
A Biblical Approach to Parenting
Copyright © 1993 by CRC Publications, 2850 Kalamazoo SE, Grand Rapids, Michigan 49560

Library of Congress Cataloging-in-Publication Data
Stolpe, Norman D., 1946-
    Who's in charge?: a biblical approach to parenting / Norman D. Stolpe.
        p.   cm.—(Issues in Christian living)
    ISBN 1-56212-029-8
    1. Parenting—Religious aspects—Christianity. 2. Discipline of children—Religious aspects—Christianity. 3. Family—Religious life. 4. Parenting—Biblical teaching. I. Title. II. Title: Who is in charge? III. Series.
BV4526.2.S745   1993
248.8'45—dc20
                                            93-9613
                                               CIP

ISBN 1-56212-029-8
9 8 7 6 5 4 3 2 1

CONTENTS

Introduction 5

One: Authority: God's Style 9
Two: To Serve Is to Take Charge 25
Three: Portable, Permanent Responsibility 43
Four: Don't Accept a Cheap Counterfeit 63
Five: Being in Charge When You Can't Be in Control 77
Six: The Conversations Continue 93

INTRODUCTION

A s I was getting close to finishing my final revisions on this material, I faced an enormous challenge to my parental authority. No, none of my children rebelliously threatened my authority or rejected my values. It was more a question of my own adequacy. Was I able to respond to a new, major crisis appropriately?

Our seventeen-year-old son, David, had had his driver's license for about three months when we visited friends in Massachusetts and left him with a family from the church. They had the car keys, but he had permission to use the car to go to his Saturday job. When Saturday came around, he left for work a little early and decided to use the extra time to explore a nearby gravel road. In his inexperience, he drove far too fast and lost control, crashing into a drainage ditch and an embankment. David was not hurt, but the car was a total loss.

That night I got a phone call. "Dad, I wrecked the car," David told me. "I'm so sorry. You trusted me, and I let you down."

I paused for a moment, almost in disbelief, trying to gather my thoughts. How was I going to respond? What were my feelings, and how would I manage them? What did David need at this point?

Dealing with that situation reminded me once again that writing and teaching about parenting in no way exempts me from its realities. Nor does my knowledge on the topic ensure that I will respond effectively at the moment of crisis. However, I discovered once again that the principles I have

5

presented in this material are constructive and reliable. I believe David would tell you that as well.

I have prepared this material as a parent and Christian educator talking to parents. My hope is that you will not just read, but that you will get involved with the whole process. Your interaction with the exercises can turn this into a conversation. I would love to chat with each parent who uses this material, swapping stories about our children and sharing all their laughs and tears.

I have learned as much from my older sons, David (17) and Jon (20) as from my studying. Let me assure you, I am still learning from Erik (6). This business of being a parent is dynamic. Every day is a new adventure. I have never been at exactly this point before, so I am utterly dependent on God's leading into a future that is unknown to me. Parenting is a perpetual act of faith.

I feel that I have learned more from the parents in the churches I have served than I can imagine having taught them. In many ways, the people who have trusted me with the joys and struggles of their families are the heroes and teachers of this material. Almost all of the illustrations that I have included are their stories, with enough details altered to protect their identity and dignity.

In my twenty-three years of ministry, I have had many conversations with parents. Over and over again, parents tell me they want discipline techniques that work. By this they usually mean that they want to do what is right for their children so they can arrive at adulthood with physical, emotional, and spiritual health. Inevitably the concept of what is "right" grows out of a viewpoint on the responsibilities of parents and children. Actually, a sound viewpoint is more helpful than a collection of techniques. Techniques are static, rigid, limited, and oriented to short-term results. Viewpoints can develop and be applied to new situations, and they tend to emphasize long-term relationships.

Perhaps the most basic viewpoint, and the one that most affects our approach to raising children, is our viewpoint on discipline. On and on the battle rages: authoritarian versus permissive. Most parents seek a route in the pathless territory between the two extremes.

The thesis of this study is that the Bible offers an alternative: *servant authority*. It is a style of parenting that is neither permissive nor authoritarian nor a compromise between the two. Servant authority gives distinctly biblical guidance to parents who are looking for direction in the lengthy but rapid journey of raising their children. The trip through this study will include some looks at other families, some examination of your own family, and some study of the Bible.

This study is not intended to be a comprehensive guide to parenting or discipline methods. Rather, those things are used as illustrations to help convey an understanding of the biblical concept of servant authority as it applies to parents. It is addressed to parents who must exercise authority, not to children who must respond to their parents' authority. Thus, you will not find admonitions for children to obey their parents here. I want to encourage parents to take responsibility for their part of the equation rather than complain about how their children handle their responsibility. I believe that, most of the time, such an action will increase parental effectiveness.

Group study is an essential ingredient in the way this material is designed. Parents can learn a lot from each other and can support each other in a fellowship of shared faith and challenge. Praying for each other is a powerful tool for building parents' confidence that they are not alone with the responsibilities of parenting. God is with them and has given them other parents as partners in the process.

If books can be distributed before the first group session, you will be able to maximize the value of your time together. Group discussions will grow out of the presentation of the sessions but should not be a rehash of the content. Instead, select issues of greatest relevance to your group and concentrate on them with an attitude of exploration. The discussion suggestions offer more than you could possibly use, so don't try to cover everything. Instead, select just a few issues that are on target for you.

While a leader is important for getting a group started and keeping it on track, this material does not assume an expert teacher. Everyone's experience is valid and valuable. The leader's job is to make sure everyone gets the greatest possible benefit from the group study.

—Norman D. Stolpe

ONE

AUTHORITY: GOD'S STYLE

This time the clash started over how precisely to interpret the rules in a family game of "Global Pursuit." I wanted to relax and just enjoy the flow of being together. I really didn't care about the technicalities of an illegal match of map pieces. However, my teenage son David wanted to play the game right. He didn't appreciate my sloppy approach to assembling the map pieces and claimed that my laziness would affect the core and outcome of the game. Of course, the issue of the game quickly faded in significance as David and I matched wills to see who was the irresistible force and who was the immovable object. The struggle was really about who's in charge.

When David and I get into one of these contests, a certain inevitability takes over, from which neither of us seems able to escape. After a while, we might as well turn on tape recorders and save ourselves the energy of the fight. Sometimes, when we have reached this point, neither of us can even remember what started it all. We know each other's lines perfectly. We've rehearsed this scene so often that we could probably switch roles without changing a word.

"David, don't make such a big deal out of it."

"My ideas just don't count around here."

"David, you're not listening to me!"

"Dad, you're so stubborn!"

"You can talk, but you can't be disrespectful."

"You're not always right, you know."

"I know, but I *am* in charge around here."

"Fine! I'll go somewhere else."

Maybe your family's conflicts are not as obvious as this, but all families experience some tension over who's in charge. I can't imagine a modern, North American parent who has not said something like, "You are my child, and I am responsible for you. As long as you live in this house, you will do as I say!" And what child has not at least thought, "You're not in charge of my life! I can hardly wait until I'm old enough to move out," and with a defiant retreat to the bedroom, "Stay out! *I'm* in charge in here!"

Find Your Flash Point

To make this study as effective as possible for you and your group, we begin with a personal inventory. Honest, confidential responses to this inventory will help you identify specific problems and questions you and others in your group have about using parental authority effectively and biblically. Those will be the areas on which you will want to focus your greatest attention in the weeks to come.

Respond to each of the following statements by checking the appropriate column.

Frequently   Sometimes   Seldom   Never

—— —— —— —— 1. I lose my temper with my children.

—— —— —— —— 2. I make threats against my children that I know I won't carry out.

—— —— —— —— 3. I am aware of inconsistencies in the way I discipline my children.

—— —— —— —— 4. "Because I said so" is the best or only reason I give my children for obeying me.

—— —— —— —— 5. My children feel free to disagree with me respectfully.

—— —— —— —— 6. My children ask for my counsel when they must make decisions.

—— —— —— —— 7. My children and I talk over our differences calmly.

—— —— —— —— 8. I tell my children I am proud of them.

—— —— —— —— 9. I enjoy being with my children.

—— —— —— —— 10. I am frustrated by my inability to make my children obey.

—— —— —— —— 11. My children embarrass me by acting up in public.

—— —— —— —— 12. My spouse and I disagree on how to handle the children.

____ ____ ____ ____ 13. I express physical affection to my children.

____ ____ ____ ____ 14. I tell my children they must submit to my authority so they can learn to submit to other authorities: police, teachers, bosses.

____ ____ ____ ____ 15. My children obey me unwillingly or under protest.

____ ____ ____ ____ 16. I feel guilty for being too hard on my children.

____ ____ ____ ____ 17. I feel guilty that I may be too easy on my children.

____ ____ ____ ____ 18. My children have temper tantrums.

____ ____ ____ ____ 19. The requests I make of my children are of primary and immediate benefit to me.

____ ____ ____ ____ 20. I confess my parental inadequacies and mistakes and ask my children for their forgiveness when I wrong them.

Nurture or Nuisance?

Sunday morning Dan dropped Mike off at toddler class before heading to worship. Four-year-old Mike whimpered and clung to his father.

"Go on now. You'll be all right. You'll have lots of fun. You're the oldest, biggest boy in the class now. Mrs. Roberts will take good care of you."

A pleasant woman in a canary smock and short brown hair reached out for Mike. "Come on in, Mike. We're building with the blocks."

As Mike passed from his father to Mrs. Roberts, he burst into tears.

"He'll be okay in a few minutes, Dan. You run along to worship. After he gets involved with the other kids, he'll start having fun and forget about crying."

With a reluctant nod, Dan turned away as Mrs. Roberts shut the door. She sat by the children who were building with the blocks and held Mike in her lap for a few minutes. When his crying seemed to subside a bit, she set him on the carpet by the blocks. He burst into screeches and screams. Immediately, Dan popped open the door. "Maybe I had better take him. He just doesn't seem to settle down here. Kathy and I haven't been to worship together more than a few times since he was born. I'm frustrated, but that just goes with caring about your kids. Maybe he'll outgrow this soon."

Mrs. Roberts picked Mike up but didn't move toward the door. "I think Mike would get used to being with the other children if he knew that you weren't outside the door waiting for him to cry. I really don't think it will take him too long to learn to fit in."

"I understand, but I don't want him to cry. He is upset and afraid. I don't want him to worry that I might abandon him or think I won't be there if he ever needs me."

"Well, you know that he settles down after calling you back three or four times. I think if he learned that he couldn't control you that way, he'd learn to get into the group right away."

"If you really think you can handle him, I guess I'll go to worship then."

"Thanks." Mrs. Roberts took Mike back to the blocks. He screamed when she set him down, but this time no father appeared at the door. After a minute or two of crying, Mike ran to the door and kicked it in a furious outburst. Still no father emerged. Mrs. Roberts quickly brought Mike back to the carpet and placed him with the other children. "Let's sit in a circle for our Bible story now. We'll finish up with the blocks later."

Mike sat right by Mrs. Roberts and tried to crawl up into her lap a couple of times as she told the Bible story and showed the pictures. He was quiet and attentive through the story, songs, and snack, but he made sure he was always close enough to Mrs. Roberts to be able to reach out and touch her. When it was time to pick up the blocks at the end of class, Mike began laughing and throwing the small ones around the room. Fearing that younger children might get hit, Mrs. Roberts tried to corral Mike. Dan appeared to retrieve Mike just as a couple of blocks sailed across the room amid peals of laughter.

"I see he adjusted. He's a big guy with quite an arm. Someday he'll be a pitcher or quarterback." Dan chuckled and turned to Mike, "Come on, All Star, it's time to go home."

Mrs. Roberts' restraining arms guided Mike to his father. As Dan dragged him down the hallway, Mike shouted repeatedly, "No! I want to play blocks!" Mrs. Roberts shook her head and heaved a sigh of relief.

Dan was concerned about nurturing Mike. He interpreted Mike's distress as a warning of impending emotional injury and wanted Mike to feel secure in his parental care. Certainly pain has no intrinsic value of its own, but by instantly coming to Mike's rescue, Dan was teaching his son that he could get his own way by causing a fuss. Dan also wanted to foster Mike's exploration of his growing abilities. But, by treating Mike's disregard of the well-being of the other children as a humorous expression of individual potential, Dan was further teaching Mike that he was the center of his universe and that others had to adapt to him. In effect, Mike was in charge of Dan.

Popular opinion would hang the label "permissive" on Dan's parenting style. It's a style that some parents gravitate toward because of their proper desires for nurture, love, encouragement, and open relationships. Other parents "fall into" the permissive style almost by default.

I was visiting some friends with a young child who seemed to wander into everything. When he disrupted our conversation, his mother gave him a cookie or something to play with. After this had happened several times, my facial expression must have given away my puzzlement at her strategy, and she commented, "I'm not a permissive parent. I'm a lazy parent."

Boot Camp at Home Base

Evangelical Christians have tended to be critical of permissive parenting, pointing to God's commands that children honor and obey their parents and to the parents' responsibility to discipline their children. However, focusing on these commands creates its own problems and often results in an emphasis on rules and penalties that casts a harsh, negative mood on parenting. It can lead parents to brace for battle when children crave support.

Peter was in high demand as a construction worker in his area. He had a reputation for giving a full day of high quality, hard work every day. He never took an extra minute for break or lunch. Whatever the weather—broiling or freezing, raining or snowing—Peter reported ready to work on time. So he had no trouble convincing a contractor to hire his seventeen-year-old son, Tim, as his partner for a summer project.

Tim's first day on the job got off to a rough start. When he wasn't at the breakfast table right on time, Peter called him. "I'll make it, Dad. All I want to eat is juice and toast."

"You'll need to eat more than that if you want enough strength to make it to lunch. Come on down. Mom's got a hot breakfast ready."

"Aw, Dad, a hot breakfast in the summer?"

"You bet! You'll need all the protein and carbs you can hold so you don't fade out like some of those young lazies who show up."

When Tim came to breakfast in shorts, sneakers, and a tank top, Peter sent him back to his room to change. "The contractor won't be impressed with your tan. Dress like you plan to work, not play. It'll help your attitude. Besides, it just makes good sense. Long sleeves, work pants, and boots are for your protection. You don't want to miss any work time because you need to bandage a cut that could have been avoided if you had dressed right."

"But, Dad, they're so hot."

"You'll just have to get used to it. It's what you have to wear if you mean business about your work."

Clothes changed and breakfast consumed, Tim was silent as they drove to the job site. "Load up all of your tools, Tim. You don't want to waste time running back and forth to the truck because you need something that's not in your tool sack."

"Won't toting all that weight slow us down?"

"Not as much as trekking to the truck. Besides, you don't make much of an impression on the boss if he sees you chasing your tools more than working with them. Getting organized is an important part of doing as much work as you can during the day. That's what they pay you for."

Peter and Tim were the first ones to meet the job supervisor. He assigned them a punch list of projects that needed to be finished in an area that was almost done. "I know you'll make sure everything is right before you sign off," he said to them. "Look it over. Any questions? If you're ready you can get started. No point waiting around for those other slowpokes."

"Wow, Dad, he respects you."

"Yeah, and I want you to build the same kind of work habits so you'll have a good reputation too."

As the day went on, Tim learned several new skills. He had thought he was pretty good at carpentry, but this detail work was a challenge. He felt he could not satisfy his father's expectations for both speed and quality at the same time. He grumbled under his breath but kept plugging along.

When they got home that night, Peter told Tim he could shower first. "Be sure to use the brush to scrub under your fingernails. You don't want to give away what your hands have been through in a day just because you don't take care of them. And check your toenails. Keep them clipped so you don't wear your socks out. You don't need sore feet to slow you down at work, and you don't need to cut into your income by buying more socks than necessary."

In just one day Tim had had about all he could take of the pressure from his dad. How would he stand up under a whole summer of this? He was sure he could never please his dad, no matter how hard he tried. At supper Tim said, "Dad, I can't keep up with you. How can I match what you've developed in nearly twenty-five years of experience? Maybe this Saturday I should look for another job that would pay nearly as well and that would be better suited to what I can do right now."

He probably could have predicted his dad's response: "You can't do that. I put my reputation on the line to get you this job. You've got to finish the summer. We made the commitment and can't back out of it now. Besides, you'll always have somebody in charge of you. Right now it's me. Even if you get to be president, you'll still have to obey the law and answer to God. You've got to learn how to take orders, or you'll have trouble all your life. Look at some of those clowns on the job—the ones who grumble about the boss and sass him. They won't get asked back. In fact, until they learn to take orders, they'll have trouble holding a job anywhere. The sooner you learn how to submit, the better. I know I'm tough on you, but there's no other way to learn how to do a job right than to do it right."

Tim was too tired to argue. Besides, he knew it wouldn't do any good. He kept quiet at supper and went to bed early to listen to music. Next summer he'd be eighteen and would have graduated from high school. He could get his own job and move out.

Rigor at the Cost of Relationships

Peter is concerned that Tim build a good reputation by learning to work hard and to obey authorities. He believes that teaching his son to perform well is more important than whether or not Tim likes him at the moment. And he's confident that someday Tim will be grateful for these lessons.

But Peter's approach has a stiff price. While parents are not primary friends of their children and need to be able to take decisive action without wavering in the face of their children's responses, Peter's tough approach has erected a wall between himself and Tim, inhibiting trusting communication. Tim submits and endures, all the while planning how to escape his dad's pressure. Furthermore, Peter's emphasis on earning one's own way becomes a practical contradiction of the New Testament's teaching of grace. Thus, though Peter's theology may be orthodox, his practice distorts the picture of God he conveys to Tim.

Peter's approach to parenting might be called "authoritarian," since it focuses so much on satisfying the demands of those in authority. This approach often fails to acknowledge the fallibility of those in positions of authority, which leads to legitimate charges of hypocrisy when children mature enough to spot the flaws. Children may assume that parents who take this approach are more concerned about what other people think than about them, their feelings and ideas, and their genuine well-being.

Under the authoritarian approach parents express love in terms of "doing what is good for you whether you like it or not," often at the expense of spontaneous expressions of affection. Such parents expect battles and insist that they win just because they are the ones in charge.

Caught in the Middle

Many parents feel torn between these two conflicting approaches to raising children: authoritarian and permissive. One parent expressed this tension well. "I am permissive with my children until I can't stand them. Then I become strongly authoritarian until I can't stand myself."[1]

Authoritarian parents, who are probably in the majority in North America, defend their hard-line approach by pointing to the immaturity and limited experience and wisdom of children. They argue that this is a world of authorities (teachers, police, bosses, etc.) and that they must teach their children to obey these authorities. Those with a knowledge of the Bible also point out that children have sinful natures that must be curbed by the parents' authority.

Permissive parents, a group that has grown considerably since World War 2, argue that children grow up best when they are freed from the problems and inhibitions of their parents. Suspicious of those in authority around them, they teach their children the value of personal freedom and self-fulfillment. They argue that too many restrictions from adults will limit the potential of the children. Those who know the Bible point to the simple faith of children and the image of God resident in each child.

In the ensuing debate, many parents harbor doubts. "Am I too strict?" "Am I too lenient?" "Where can I find a model of parenthood that really fits my needs and the needs of my children?" Confusion over the unbiblical philosophies of authoritarian and permissive parenthood (and the impossible attempt to find a balance between them) poses some practical problems for parents. Some of the most common of these problems are listed below. Most parents will identify with at least one of them. By being aware of the problems, parents can focus energy on the areas of greatest need.

Identifying Your Discomfort

Each statement listed below characterizes a problem area that grows out of the tension over parental authority. Read through the list and select the three that are most troublesome for you. Then number them 1 (most difficult), 2, or 3 (least difficult).

_____ 1. After I discipline my child, I wonder if I really took the best course of action.

_____ 2. If my friends are around when I discipline my child, I feel they are critical of how I handle the situation.

_____ 3. When my child accuses me of being unfair, I sometimes wonder if he or she is right.

_____ 4. I feel confused when I read a book or article or listen to someone speak about how to raise children.

_____ 5. I feel sorry for parents who are just starting to raise their children now.

_____ 6. I often am unsure how to handle specific situations with my children.

_____ 7. I have a hard time responding to my children consistently.

_____ 8. I am troubled that others seem to discipline their children differently than I do.

_____ 9. I feel offended when someone makes a suggestion or observation that seems to question the way I raise my children.

_____ 10. I change my mind (or want to change my mind) after I have told my children my decisions.

Now examine the three items you have checked and complete this sentence:

My greatest need in exercising parental authority is . . .

Authority's Adhesive

That so many parent-child struggles end with the impasse of the parent insisting, "Because I told you so," or "Because I'm your parent," and the child retorting (silently if not aloud), "You don't run my life," or "Just wait until I leave home," indicates the importance of identifying the source of authority. As long as parents and children struggle over who's in charge, they are left with the subjective answer of "whoever has enough power to take charge." In the long run, children will always win that war. They grow up and move out. They are free to choose the terms of their adult relationship with their parents.

What they need is a new answer to the question of who's in charge. Both parents and children need someone to be in charge who has an in-

16

dependent right to authority and a believable commitment to the best interests of both children and parents. The one who is in charge needs to provide objective, dependable standards that apply equally to parents and children. The one who is in charge needs to extend unconditional love that offers merciful acceptance without compromising expectations. So the obvious identity of the one who is rightfully in charge is God.

Scripture indicates that God is the source of all kinds of authority. Though certainly not following the pattern of modern corporate management, God allows people to act as his agents by delegating authority to them. It may be authority in the world, such as in government (Rom. 13:1) or employment (Col. 3:23-24). The Bible never naively assumes any righteousness on the part of rulers or employers but suggests that though these may be godless, wicked people, they are still God's servants acting on God's behalf (1 Pet. 2:13-17; Isa. 44:28; Habakkuk). That God is the source of worldly authority imposes standards of justice on those who exercise it as well as on those who must live under it.

The New Testament speaks more frequently about God as the source of authority in the church (Matt. 18:18; 1 Cor. 5:3-4, 6:6; 1 Thess. 5:12-13; Titus 2:15, 3:1). Though authority in the church, as in the world, comes from God, a marked shift occurs in the quality God expects of this authority. While worldly rulers may sometimes be godless, church authorities must consistently reveal the character of God in the way they exercise their authority.

Parental authority, too, finds its source in God. God's character becomes the measure of how parents use their authority, because God has delegated his authority to them. Scripture presents God to us as a father (Matt. 5:45; John 1:14; Rom. 8:15). As father, God serves his children (Ps. 68:5; Matt. 7:11; Luke 15:20-32). We can understand God's service in terms of his activity as creator, judge, and redeemer.

God as Creator

God created people in his own image (Gen. 1:26-27) and delegated to them the authority (Gen. 1:28) to care for the earth (Gen. 2:5, 15). Thus, the distinctive authority that God intended for people precedes the fall and is not a response to sin. It is this sort of authority God calls believers to in the church and in the family.

When God created people, he made them "authority bearing creatures"[2] who are able to have relationships with God and with other people. Thus, people are able to represent God in human relationships, including authority relationships. Parents are given the authority to represent God to their children and to enable these young ones to reflect the image of God.

The words "subdue" and "rule" (Gen. 1:28) are usually thought of as the authority words in God's commission to humans. These terms were further defined as people were placed in the garden to care for it (Gen. 2:5, 15). God's commission gave people charge or authority over the garden, but that authority was to be exercised in a specific way. The word often translated "till" literally means "serve," and is translated that way in most other Old Testament occurrences.[3] Thus, people were given authority to *serve* the garden according to the creation commission.

When our first son, Jon, was born, we became aware of this creative authority. We learned to pay attention to his needs and tried to respond to them as promptly as possible. If he needed food, sleep, or a diaper change, we were ready to serve him. Though these tasks were not always "fun," "serving" our child and celebrating each new milestone in his life was hardly an imposition on us. It was the way we used our positions of authority to affirm our son's worth and ability. At first, we made almost all decisions for him: what to wear, when and what to eat, and when to sleep. These were expressions of our creative authority, which still mark his habits and identity now as a college student. Even though he lives apart from us now, he phones home almost every week to report his academic and social delights and pains, and I sense in those calls a craving for the security and affirmation of our creative authority.

God as Judge

With the coming of sin, the image of God was marred and distorted in people. Authority was corrupted. People began using God-given authority to oppress others and to achieve selfish ends. Authority became a device for controlling rather than serving, and without it anarchy ruled. God, the source of authority, was forgotten or given only casual lip-service.

So God acted again, this time as judge. He gave the law through Moses. He sent prophets to warn of impending judgment, which came with the destruction of ancient Israel. Ultimately, God executed judgment on Jesus Christ on the cross.

The law is the chief, ongoing expression of God's activity as judge. God's law points out the failure of sinful people to either recognize God's authority (direct or delegated) or to exercise delegated authority as God intended—in service to those over whom one has authority. Since it does expose sin (Rom. 7; James 1:25), "the Law teaches us what we are to do and not to do. . . . The law is to be preached to impenitent sinners (including the 'flesh' of Christians)."[4] The law dispels any illusions of self-righteousness.

In a fallen world, the law becomes a tool of authority. It serves to define who is in submission and who is not. It meets our judgments on those who disobey. Interestingly, it also stimulates rebellion and resistance (Rom. 7:7-11, 21). It is the mirror (James 1:23-25) that illuminates and reflects the shortcomings of sinners so they can repent. It is the schoolmaster (Gal. 3:24) who guides the child to maturity, responsibility, and freedom. So even as judge, God acts on behalf of his children, for their benefit rather than his own.

Our church has a policy of providing "scholarship" help to young people so no one has to miss a retreat or other special event for lack of money. One year as winter retreat time was approaching, a mother and father took me aside privately to talk about their daughter. "We don't want you to give Carol a scholarship for this retreat. She had a good summer job and has been working part-time since school started. She has earned plenty of money to pay for the retreat, but she has been running around with her friends, eating out, and buying a lot of clothes at the mall—far more than she needs. We think she needs to face the reality of her spending and not get bailed out at the last minute. We are going to explain our decision to her tonight and would like to know that you will back us up."

Though I don't like to keep kids away from events that could be of spiritual benefit to them, I agreed with these parents. They were acting in the role of judge to confront their daughter with the consequences of her irresponsible spending. And they kept the issue objective (wanting money for the retreat), rather than becoming judgmental or demeaning.

God as Redeemer

To understand parental authority only in terms of God's activity as creator is overly optimistic and can lead to an unbiblical permissiveness. On the other hand, to approach parental authority only from God's activity as judge is unduly pessimistic and can lead to unbiblical authoritarianism. For a complete and adequate perspective on parental authority, God's activity in Christ as redeemer is the key.

Redemptive authority is able to accommodate the tragic paradox of being made in the image of God but still revolting against the good God wants for us. It accounts for our complete dependence on an external rescue and the marvelous potential of being called to serve in the kingdom of God. It is the hope for restoration in the face of failure that is evident in Jesus' words, "Go now and leave your life of sin" (John 8:11). It is God's call to a new life in the Spirit (1 Cor. 6:9-11).

When parents use their authority redemptively, they are able to comfort and support children who are in pain from the wrong someone else has done to them or who are feeling guilty about their own wrong behavior. Redemptive authority conveys the message of God's mercy: "This hurt and the wrong that caused it is not the last word. God offers hope for healing and a new direction." Part of that hope is the promise of release from the prison of past patterns.

For example, a parent may say, "Just because you've gotten into the habit of lying to try to get out of trouble doesn't mean you are doomed to continue that way. God wants you to really start trying to be truthful. And God will forgive you for lying." This might be a good time to read Psalm 32 together and talk about how good it feels to be forgiven. Such a conversation could go on to explore ways parents and children can help each other be more open and honest. Such a strategy in no way encourages or makes light of wrong behavior; rather, it stimulates the practical reinforcement of right behavior. It also frees children from the guilt feelings that damage self-worth and inhibit positive change.

Lisa was fighting back tears as she talked to her mother. "I'm sorry I let you down. I know I promised to baby-sit Jeremy after school while you went shopping. I was having so much fun at Kathy's that I forgot you needed me."

"Yes, it was harder to get the groceries with a three-year-old. He didn't want to ride in the cart, but that was the only way I could keep track of him. Also, I was worried about you, since I didn't know where you were."

"I know I've been forgetting to tell you where I am after school a lot more this year. I don't mean to, but I just get involved in what I'm doing. Everything seems okay to me, so I forget that you might be worried."

"I know you're getting older and can do a lot more on your own now, but you still have to follow through on your responsibilities to the rest of the family. I want to help you learn how to handle your new freedoms and to be considerate of others at the same time."

"I know I messed up. Am I hopeless?"

"No, you're not hopeless. I forgive you. I have a couple of ideas that might help. What if you told me your after-school plans at breakfast and I wrote them on the chalkboard by the phone? If I need you that afternoon, I'll remind you at breakfast, and you can write it in your assignment book."

"I like the assignment book idea, but my friends and I usually make our plans when we're walking home in the afternoon. What if I gave you a list of my friends' phone numbers, so you know where to call me?"

"That might be a help, but I don't want to have to guess which friend you're with or have to make several phone calls."

"What if I phoned from where I am as soon as I got there?"

"Maybe we could try that after a couple of weeks, if you've been consistent in letting me know your plans in advance for a while. But for now, decide among your friends today where you will go tomorrow."

"That's not what I'd like, but I guess I have to go with it since I messed up today. You'll see—I'll learn and you'll be able to trust me."

Power to Parent

Parents who recognize that God is the source of their authority have much more power at their disposal than parents who must rely on force to support their authority. This power is released by parents pointing out to their children that all authority comes from God. Thinking in terms of God's activity as creator, judge, and redeemer will suggest many ways and situations for recognizing God's authority as the source of human authority.

The brief examples below represent situations in which parents may tell their children of God's authority. In response to each one, write a one- or two-sentence reply or comment that parents could make to their children

20

that would point to God as the source of authority. Also indicate whether this reply shows God's activity as creator, judge, or redeemer.

Sample:

At supper Saturday evening twelve-year-old John said, "Dad, you promised I could help you service the car today, but you did it all by yourself."

Parents' response: "Oh no! I forgot about that. I could have used your help too. I'm sorry. Will you forgive me?"

_____ creator _____ judge __X__ redeemer

1. A teary-eyed, four-year-old Jill creeps up behind Mom, hugs her knees, and whines, "I just broke the vase in the living room. I'm sorry. Are you going to scream at me?"
   Parent's response:

   _____ creator _____ judge _____redeemer

2. Seventeen-year-old Kathy has the lead in the school play. At Monday's supper she says, "Dad, Mr. Hudson, the drama teacher, said today that we'll have a reception for the families of the cast after the play Saturday night. I know we were planning a special party just with our family, but I'd rather have you all come to the one at school. Would that be okay?"
   Parent's response:

   _____ creator _____ judge _____redeemer

3. The discussion of family vacation plans has boiled down to two alternatives, both of which are acceptable to Mom and Dad. However, fourteen-year-old Dan and sixteen-year-old Karen don't seem to be able to reach an agreement, and neither is willing to compromise. Mom feels that all the squabbling is spoiling the fun of having a vacation. Dan says, "Karen, why don't you just stay home and go to summer school instead of wrecking the vacation for all of us?" Karen answers, "Why don't you? You're the stubborn one!"
   Parent's response:

   _____ creator _____ judge _____redeemer

4. Dad has just been stopped by the police for traveling twelve miles per hour over the speed limit. As the officer walks away, thirteen-year-old Joan says, "That policeman is sure dumb to give you a ticket."
   Parent's response:

   _____ creator _____ judge _____redeemer

Now think back over your interaction with *your* children in the past week, paying special attention to the times you have used your authority. Think of ways you did or could have told your children about God's authority as creator, judge, and redeemer. In a sentence or two, write what you did or could say to your child.

creator:

judge:

redeemer:

Suggestions for Group Session

Opening

Read the introduction to this course. Whether you are a group leader or participant, you will find that understanding the expectations presented there will increase the value of the group experience. The suggestions for this first session assume that people in the group have read the material and have completed the exercises before coming. However, some may not have gotten books, so you will want to be sure everyone has received a copy before starting the discussion.

Getting acquainted is very important at the beginning of any endeavor in which people will be sharing sensitive feelings and struggles. The hope is that this group can be a supportive fellowship for parents. If that is to happen, trust must be cultivated from the very beginning. Go around the group, asking each person to introduce himself or herself. Even when people already think they know each other, they usually discover new things about each other in a group like this. People may wish to tell the group one interesting characteristic about each of their children as part of their introductions.

Before actually starting on the work of the course, develop a list of group expectations or goals. Tell why you are taking this course and what you hope to gain from the experience. If you list the group's basic ideas on sheets of newsprint, they can be posted in the meeting room each time you gather. This will help focus attention on the areas of greatest interest and value to those in the group. Obviously, there is more here than can be covered fully in six one-hour sessions, so you will need to decide where to focus your attention. Such a list will help with that. It will also help all of you recognize what you have accomplished by the end of the course.

With these preliminary procedures taken are of, take some time to pray for your study together as a group. One person can do this on behalf of the group, or, if people are comfortable with it, a group prayer time is valuable.

Pray that God will speak to and through your group and that the Holy Spirit will work in group discussion. Also pray that God will meet the needs of all of the parents and children in the group. Thank God for the opportunity to learn together and to support each other.

For Discussion

1. To further identify the issues that will take priority attention for this group, everyone should scan their responses to the Personal Inventory (p. 10) and Identifying Your Discomfort (p. 16). Pay particular attention to the sentence completion at the end of Identifying Your Discomfort: "My greatest need in exercising parental authority is . . ." Discuss as a group the "hottest," most relevant topics that lie ahead for this course. You may wish to list these on sheets of newsprint as well. Another way to get at this is to discuss answers to the following question: In what ways do I want to be different after completing this course?

2. None of us grew up in a vacuum. We were shaped by our parents, sometimes in imitation and sometimes in reaction. At times we are aware of their influence; at other times it is unconscious. Tell the group something about the way your parents used authority while you were growing up that affects the way you use authority with your children.

3. Discuss with the group these four perspective questions on styles of authority. Listing them on a chalkboard divided into four columns or on four sheets of newsprint may be helpful.
   a. What benefits of authoritarian parenting would you like to claim?

   b. What benefits of permissive parenting would you like to claim?

   c. What liabilities of authoritarian parenting would you like to avoid?

   d. What liabilities of permissive parenting would you like to avoid?

4. Read Genesis 1:28. In what ways does God's delegation of authority to the human race at creation affect all kinds of human authority? What are the common threads that tie all authority together? What happens when human authority is abused or used to rebel against God? What does this say about the ways authority is used and responded to by those who trust God and those who don't?

5. Compare and contrast how authority properly works in the world, in the church, and in the family. What are the similarities, and what are the differences?

6. Read Galatians 3:19, 23-25. How does the way God uses the law help us as parents know how to use our parental authority to guide our children toward redemption?

7. Review your responses to Power to Parent (page 21). Then divide into three equal-sized groups, each of which will focus on one of God's authority roles: creator, judge, redeemer. In each group, identify ways you as parents have reflected this role as you have exercised parental authority. Then regather in one large group and discuss the importance of balancing all three roles in your families. What do we accomplish by seeking such a balance? In what areas is the balance most difficult to achieve? What do you think would help you become more balanced?

8. Brainstorm ways to let your children know in a positive way that God is the source of your authority as parents and that you want to reflect God as you exercise your parental authority.

   Brainstorming means that you want to develop as many ideas as possible in the time allowed. Do not discuss or evaluate the ideas. A "bad" one may suggest a "good" one a minute later! Work as quickly as possible, and encourage everyone to participate fully.

   For this brainstorming activity, set a specific time frame and stick to it. If, for example, you decide to work for ten minutes, you will probably find that the last three minutes are the most productive. Designate one person to write all of the ideas on a chalkboard or newsprint pad.

Closing

Read Psalm 32 aloud. Meditate in silence for several minutes on the wonder of God's forgiving grace. Close with sentence prayers from the group, expressing thanks for God's grace to us and to our children.

[1]Gordon, Thomas. *Parent Effectiveness Training.* New York: New American Library, 1970, p. 162.
[2]Vos, Clarence. "Biblical Perspectives on Authority in the Home." *FIT Instructor's Manual.* Grand Rapids, MI: Pine Rest Life Enrichment Center, 1974, pp. 24-32.
[3]Harris, R. Laird, Gleason L. Archer, Jr., Bruce K. Waltke. *Theological Wordbook of the Old Testament.* Chicago: Moody Press, 1980, page 639.
[4]Gaulke, Earl. *You Can Have a Family Where Everybody Wins.* St. Louis, MO: Concordia Press, 1975, page 24.

TWO

TO SERVE IS TO TAKE CHARGE

Every summer for the past several years I have gone with our church's high school youth group on their work camp experience. The year that my oldest son, Jon, graduated from high school, we went to Syracuse, New York and worked with the Habitat for Humanity project there.

What I especially remember about that week are the group Bible studies we had after work each evening. We spent some time talking together about our citizenship in the kingdom of God and the hope and dignity it brings us. And we wondered together about what implications that citizenship has for our everyday relationships in the here and now. How should boys and girls treat each other? How should we feel about the people in the poor neighborhood where we were working, especially those who would live in the houses we were building? How could we respond with respect to people who were different than we were? What did this mean in our family relationships: brothers and sisters, children and parents?

Out of these discussions emerged a theme: We noted that while our human relationships and roles are temporary (Mark 12:25), our relationships as equal brothers and sisters in the kingdom are permanent and eternal. Friend and friend, husband and wife, teacher and student, leader and follower, boss and worker, pastor and parishioner, parent and child—all of these eventually fade into being sisters and brothers together with Jesus in the kingdom of God.

At the end of our week in Syracuse, each person wrote a "nurture note" to each of the others in the group. When I read the note from my son

Jon, I realized just how significant an impact our Bible study theme had had on group members. He wrote in part,

> I may be going to college, but I'm not leaving the family. I thank you for the responsibilities you have given me. Thanks for leading me to God.
>
> Your son and future brother,
>
> Jon

That was a good reminder to me that as a Christian parent, my job is not so much to produce a good son (or daughter) as to nurture eternal sisters and brothers. My responsibility is to be God's agent, cultivating in my children the values and habits of the kingdom and the character of the King.

This kingdom perspective gives awesome significance to my parental role. I am entrusted with the care and nurture of growing citizens of God's eternal kingdom. It is also a humbling reminder of the transitory nature of the parenting task and the temporary nature of the parent-child relationship.

Don't Look Back to Eden

I need to look ahead to what the kingdom will be in its fullness to accurately understand who my children are. The alternative is to look back to Eden, but that distorts the picture by limiting the view. If I assume my children are innocent and inherently good (their pre-fall condition), I will tend to be a permissive parent who sees little need for discipline. On the other hand, if I focus on the fall and see my children as fundamentally sinful, I will tend to be authoritarian and will run the risk of failing to recognize the work of God's image and grace in them.

Looking ahead and visualizing my children as citizens in the glorious kingdom can prevent me from falling into either of these extremes. If I recognize that my children and I are all people Christ died to redeem, I can fully account for our shared sinfulness while maintaining an optimistic, expectant attitude. As the one in charge, I have the responsibility to exercise the tools of authority to cultivate kingdom qualities. Since I know that this role is temporary, I do not have to feel threatened when my children challenge my authority. In anticipating our eternal equality, I can celebrate the times when I learn from them, when I must ask for as well as give forgiveness, when they make mature choices independent of my direct input.

I am humbled that my divine parental commission makes me a partner with Christ in preparing people he has redeemed for service in the kingdom of God. Raising children makes me a servant of Christ and steward of the authority that belongs to him. I tingle with awe at the thought of what God is making of my children and what place they will take in the kingdom.

Kingdom Catalog for Your Children

The kingdom perspective is like spectacles that help me see more clearly what is taking place in my children's lives. When I recognize traits and patterns that are consistent with the kingdom of God, I want to encourage, reinforce, and highlight them. On the other hand, I want to discourage, extinguish, and minimize traits and patterns that are contrary to God's kingdom. As my sons mature, I want to be alert for opportunities to sample and savor our coming relationship as kingdom brothers (or sisters, for those of you with daughters).

Take a few minutes to reflect on the best qualities in *your* children. Then describe or list the ways you see God building the values of the kingdom in each of them. Complete this exercise as an act of faith that God is at work in the lives of the children of believing parents, and that we can look for evidence of that work expecting to find it (Acts 2:38-39; 1 Cor. 7:14; 2 Tim. 1:5). If you need some input on qualities of the kingdom of God, try looking at the fruit of the Spirit (Gal. 5:22-23), the Beatitudes (Matt. 5:3-10), or the rest of the Sermon on the Mount (Matt. 5-7).

What qualities of the kingdom of God can I identify in _____?
(name of child)

What qualities of the kingdom of God can I identify in _____?
(name of child)

What qualities of the kingdom of God can I identify in _____?
(name of child)

What qualities of the kingdom of God can I identify in _____?
(name of child)

What qualities of the kingdom of God can I identify in _____?
(name of child)

What qualities of the kingdom of God can I identify in _____?
(name of child)

Take a few minutes before going on with your reading to thank God for working in the lives of your children.

Which Nature Is in Charge?

When our youngest son, Erik, was starting first grade, he had a tough time adjusting to the longer school day and increased work load. He came home tired, and for the first couple of weeks in September was unusually grouchy at supper time. One night when he was particularly testy, he an-

27

nounced that he was leaving our family and moving to Illinois to live with his grandparents.

Later that evening—after eating, finishing homework, and bathing—he curled up with me on the couch to read a Bible story and the next chapter of C. S. Lewis' *Voyage of the Dawn Treader.* When the reading was finished, he snuggled his head tight against my chest, slipped his arms around me, and said, "Dad, I love you." I knew that that was not the time to remind him of his angry announcement earlier in the evening—his "old self." It was time to revel in his "new self" and to enjoy the warmth of the moment.

One of the challenges of being partners with Christ in the redemption business is that we must contend with ongoing sinfulness as well as gloriously emerging righteousness. The New Testament describes believers as having two natures (Eph. 4:22-24; Col. 3:9-10). Focusing on the "old nature," as is the tendency of authoritarian parents, is the trap of judgment that cannot stimulate maturity. Permissiveness, on the other hand, inadvertently brings out the unbridled selfishness of the "old nature."

In Christian families, parents use their authority to draw out and build up the "new nature" of their children. Parents and children, then, can relate to each other as one redeemed person to another. They recognize the great gift of God's image with which they were created. They both know that the other is a rebellious, disobedient sinner. They both appreciate the grace and forgiveness that God has extended to redeem the other.

As believing parents we dare not presume upon God's grace for our children or take it for granted. Indeed, one of the most profound privileges and responsibilities of redemptive parental authority is presenting the gospel to our children. God faithfully keeps covenant with the children of believing parents, but God also calls parents to be faithful in introducing their children to Jesus Christ and inviting them to repent and trust in him.

A mother of preschool children was feeling frustrated and useless. Her days seemed to be endless routines of diapers, meals, and cleaning. She voiced her discontent in an adult Sunday school class. "I love my children, but I feel like they are preventing me from having a meaningful ministry for God. I feel like I should be using my gifts to evangelize people."

One of the other people in the group shared a liberating, empowering insight. "Have you thought that right now, God may be calling you to evangelize your children? Who knows what God has planned for them? Tell them how to love, trust, and follow Jesus now while they are close to you. Expect God to do great things with them when they leave you. And be prepared for new ministries God will give you as your children become more independent."

The tone of the comment was just right, encouraging and freeing rather than restraining or condemning.

Every baptism and every celebration of the Lord's Supper is an opportunity to rehearse the gospel with your children. Don't be afraid to ask your children questions that encourage them to respond to God's redeeming work in Christ. "What does it mean to you that Jesus died for your sins?" "What does it mean to you to be forgiven?" "What does it mean to you to trust Jesus?" If such conversation is comfortable for you and your children, you may just find that one day your children will want you to help them with a prayer of faith something like this: "Heavenly Father, I know I have done wrong. I trust Jesus to forgive me. I want to do what Jesus wants and live with him forever. Thank you that he died on the cross and rose to life again so this can happen. In Jesus' name. Amen."

Kingdom Construction

The summer before our middle son, David, started high school, our church youth-group work camp was in Coatsville, Pennsylvania. The houses we worked on there were immediately adjacent to a large, deteriorating public housing project. When we started work each day, many children from the project gathered to watch and to offer help. David got to know several of them and tried to involve them in some of the smaller projects to which he was assigned, especially clearing brush where new foundations were to be dug.

One afternoon a couple of the kids tired of working and started "fencing" with some sticks. As they charged back and forth, they stumbled over some younger children playing with toy cars on the sidewalk. One little boy started crying, and the older ones ran away. I became aware of what had happened when I saw David walking up the hill toward the housing development holding a tearful little boy's hand, and I asked David's work crew where he was going. "Oh, he's taking that kid home. He got hurt when those bigger kids ran over him while they were playing."

Apprehensively, I waited for David to return. He was heading into unknown territory. Would the boy's mother thank or blame him . . . if he could even find her? How would the neighbors respond to this strange teenager with a crying child in tow? How would David respond if anyone challenged him?

My fears were unnecessary. David returned, beaming. "I'm proud of you," I told him. "You took charge of a problem and did what was right. You thought more about someone else's welfare than your own. Risking the unfamiliar to serve someone else was your faith at work. You have learned an important lesson in Christian ministry today."

Our parental authority becomes a tool for reinforcing the values of the kingdom of God. We can help our children recognize these urges as the working of the Holy Spirit in their lives. We serve both Christ and our children by making connections between everyday life and the present and coming kingdom of God.

Think about times you have been able to do this for your children.

In what ways have you sought to affirm kingdom values in your children?

In what ways have you tried to limit patterns in your children's lives that are inconsistent with the kingdom of God?

As your children mature, what steps do you think you might take to recognize your ultimate relationship as equal brothers and sisters in the kingdom of God?

Upside Down, Inside Out, and Backwards

God has used his authority as creator, judge, and redeemer for the benefit of people. As creator, God gives people his image, the basis for human dignity. As judge, God gives the law to bring us to repentance and to guide us to mature, responsible freedom (James 1:25). As redeemer, God paid the high price for our salvation through the sacrifice of Jesus Christ.

God expects people of faith to follow that pattern, using their authority to serve each other. Humble service is the most characteristic quality of biblical authority, the quality that sets biblical authority apart from all human philosophies of authority.

In Matthew 20:25-28 and Mark 10:42-45, Jesus speaks to his disciples in unmistakable terms about the sort of authority he expects from them. He boldly repudiates the popular understandings of authority that lead to permissiveness and authoritarianism. Then he institutes a whole new approach to authority that is a paradox, if not a contradiction, of all human thinking about authority. According to Jesus, authority is service.

But Jesus doesn't stop at *telling* his disciples that authority is service. He goes on to demonstrate it to them. He specifically tells his followers that washing their feet (John 13:3-17) is an act of authority. When he starts, he identifies himself not only as their leader, but as God, the source of all authority (verse 3). After washing their feet, Jesus explains that what he has done is to be understood in terms of his lordship (vv. 13-16). To communicate his intent for authority, the incarnate God of the universe rendered the most lowly service of washing feet. This lesson in servant authority came just hours before Christ's ultimate service to humanity on Calvary and the subsequent victory of his authority over death on Easter.

Jesus knew that presenting authority as humble service was an incomprehensible affront to the sinful ordering of human society: autocratic governments, dictatorial pastors, privileged executives, overbearing husbands, authoritarian parents. Yet the clear teaching and example of Jesus is that authority is service. The task of those in authority is to serve those for whom they are responsible. Anything else is no longer authority but "lording it over," which Jesus specifically condemns. Thus, parents are to use the authority delegated to them by God to *serve* their children.

Much of this probably sounds like parents must surrender their authority and power. That this is not true is the mystery and strength of biblical authority. Human authority must rely on force and coercion because it has no other basis for fulfilling its objectives, and its objectives then tend to be self-serving rather than other-serving. In contrast, Paul writes of overcoming evil with good and heaping coals of fire on one's enemies by doing them good (Rom. 12:17-21). In much the same way, this servant approach to parental authority has behind it a power much greater than any force that humans might exert.

Parents need not appeal to their own power, but can draw on the power of God's love in Christ (2 Cor. 5:20). Their word commands respect because it rests on something larger than the parents themselves, because it is directed to the good of the child, and because it is spoken with mutual respect from one redeemed sinner to another.

Parents who exercise servant authority are not weak and opinionless. They care deeply and hold strong convictions. In fact, these parents are so strong and secure that they are not threatened either as persons or parents by a rebellious or insolent child. Because God's ways are often the reverse of human ways, the servant parent is the steward of God's power.

The summer before Janet started fourth grade, her mother took her for a sundae after supper. "I think you're getting old enough for some new responsibilities. You're already doing a good job at this year's list: setting and clearing the supper table, loading the dishwasher, and making your bed. I'd like you to choose one or two things to learn this summer that will help you to take care of some more of your own needs. I've thought of a couple ideas: making your lunch before you go to bed and running the washing machine. Maybe you have some other ideas."

"Well, I have sometimes wished I knew how to iron or sew. Then I wouldn't have to wait as long if I wanted to wear something in the dirty clothes basket. I also think it might be fun to learn to paint my room and make my own curtains."

After talking about the implications of these possibilities, Janet and her mother settled on washing, ironing, and sewing for the summer project. Mother would teach Janet the skills over the summer, and the week before school started they would decide exactly how much Janet had learned and could continue doing during the school year. They agreed that Janet had to do full loads in the washer, which meant washing, drying, and folding some clothes for other members of the family as well as taking care of her own. They also decided that just before Christmas or Easter vacation they would talk again about painting Janet's room.

As you might expect, Mother experienced some frustrating moments during the summer teaching process. Some things lay in the dryer too long, and ironing out the wrinkles was not easy. Janet got tired of the learning sessions, especially if she didn't get it quite right. But Mother kept reaffirming the goal of the freedom that would come when Janet could care for her own clothes.

By the end of August, Janet decided she was ready to be in charge of the care of her own clothing. Mother agreed, reminding Janet that she was willing to help whenever Janet had a problem and asked for assistance. Around Halloween, Janet was wearing some things too many days, and wearing some things unironed. Mother had to work hard not to say anything. After all, Janet was the one who wanted to be free of depending on Mother. By Thanksgiving, Janet was handling the schedule smoothly. In January, Janet had the flu for a few days, and Mother took over for a couple of weeks, but only after asking Janet if that was all right. The painting decision was deferred to Easter break.

Janet's mother used her authority to serve Janet. She took the initiative to propose another step of learning and responsibility. She suggested ideas and was open to Janet's input. Mother paid the price and made the effort to do the teaching over the summer. Once Janet officially took on the responsibility, Mother had the self-discipline not to nag, belittle, or take back the responsibility. Mother made herself available to help, problem-solve, and even fill in as needed, but respected Janet's ownership of the new jobs. By doing so, Mother not only built mature responsibility habits in Janet, but she also bolstered Janet's self-esteem.

Working from a secure authority power base, Mother was Janet's servant, helping her grow rather than enlisting Janet as a laborer to ease Mother's work load. Ultimately, of course, the change did mean less work for Mother, but that was not the motivation.

Attitude Is More Important than Technique

How can the ideal of servant authority be approached? Where do parents start to be effective authorities by serving their children? As important as practical behavior is, it must rest on proper attitudes.

Humility probably heads the list, as it permeates every aspect of this study. A genuine desire to serve is the driving force behind all effective authority. As parents, we must recognize and respect the dignity and personhood of our children.

Example is another important ingredient. Children learn how to respond to their parents' authority by observing how their parents respond to those in authority over them. Parents who chafe and rebel against the authority of those over them will find that their children will also chafe and rebel against their authority. Parents who seek to subvert or circumvent the authority of those over them will find their children subverting and circumventing their authority. Only parents who recognize that their authority is not absolute, that its source is in God, can biblically exercise authority over their children.

Hank sat down with Julie to go over the classes she wanted to take when she started high school next year. "Explain to me what you have to do on this form here."

"Well, basically, I need to show whether I want business, general, or college-prep tracks. That choice actually decides most of the classes. I do need to choose between art and music for my elective, though. And if I choose college prep, I take a different track in science than I would with the business or general tracks. Everybody gets gym."

"Well, what were you planning to sign up for?"

"I guess I always expected to try for college. That's what you want, isn't it? Sometimes all that stuff scares me though."

"Sure, I want you to be able to go to college if that's what you really want. Sounds like you're not so sure."

"Making such big decisions when I'm fourteen years old is tough. How am I supposed to know what's best for the rest of my life?"

"You don't have to figure it all out now."

"It would be easier if you just told me the right thing to do."

"I don't really know what is best all of the time. My job is to help you make your own decisions."

"I just don't know, Dad. I've never gone to high school before."

"I've never had a daughter go to high school before either. I probably feel as excited and as afraid as you do."

"But you went to high school. You always seem to know what's right to do."

"Well, yes, I went to high school, but I wasn't paying as much attention then. Besides, it's a lot harder to help someone else, especially somebody I care about as much as you. I want to steer you right, and I don't always know what to tell you."

"It seems to me that you usually do a pretty good job."

"I do trust that God will guide us, even when we don't know what's best. I read the Bible and pray. Every day I ask God to help me do what is good for you. Even when I mess up, I trust God to fix things. I wouldn't want to be a parent without knowing that God was really the one in charge of me and our family."

Many parents who feel awed and sometimes frightened by their parental responsibilities never let their children in on such feelings. Rather, they give their children a sense of parental omnipotence and omniscience. To do this is to usurp the authority of God. Parents should freely tell their children that they have authority only because God has called them to this responsibility and not because of any special knowledge or power of their own. Parents must stand ready to be taught by their children without being threatened by the process.

To serve in authority, parents must seek the interests of their children and not just their own interests (Phil. 2:3-4). Some parents make the mistake of thinking that what seems best to them and their peers will necessarily be best for their children. And they subtly or overtly influence and manipulate their children to live up to their expectations. This is not to say that parents do not have a better understanding of their children's best interests than do the children. Often they do. But parents must humbly recognize their own fallibility and not lean too heavily on the inadequate explanation, "I know what's best for you." One does not impose service on another.

A group of mothers of high schoolers gathered in the foyer after worship. Jim Jenkins spoke to his mother as he walked by with Rick. "Mom, I'm going to stop at home and change clothes. Then I'll go over to Rick's. We'll grab lunch and go shoot some baskets with the guys at the middle school."

They were already out the door before Mrs. Jenkins could respond, "I guess that's all right. Come home in time to get your homework done for Monday." She turned back to her friends. "They just can't seem to get enough of each other. It's so hard to have a relaxed family Sunday anymore."

This exchange prompted the mothers to voice their pet complaints about their teenage children. Mrs. Schmidt shook her head as she said, "I just can't get Cindy to dress up for church. She wants to wear jeans all the time."

Mrs. Moyer chimed in, "Ever since Jerry started eighth grade, he slouches in worship. He slides down until his head rests on the back of the pew with his feet stuck straight out in front of him."

"I get the feeling they try to embarrass us," sighed Mrs. Jenkins.

Mrs. Martin had listened quietly. Her youngest child, Jill, was a high school senior. Later she told me, "I didn't want to say too much, since my children are basically grown, but I was always happy if they wanted to be in worship and with the church youth group. That seemed more important to me than fashion or posture. Sometimes I'm sure people wondered about what was wrong with me when my children did some of their silly things at church. But I'm glad they felt comfortable enough to make their best friends here."

Your Response

The idea that authority equals service is new to many people, and applying it to parenting may at first seem impractical. However, if you have been following carefully from the beginning, you probably have some emotional responses to what you have been reading. The following questions will help you get some of those emotions out in the open for you to examine before going on. Check the appropriate space to indicate your answer to each question. If you are working alone and will not be discussing your answers in a group, explore briefly why you feel as you do. Remember that all of your emotions are valid feelings, so no answer is wrong.

1. When I think that the only authority I have as a parent is the authority God gives me, I feel
   ___ a. relieved.
   ___ b. awed.
   ___ c. frightened.
   ___ d. inadequate.
   ___ e. offended.

   Why?

2. The prospect of asking forgiveness of my child
   ___ a. humiliates me.
   ___ b. scares me.
   ___ c. reassures me.
   ___ d. insults me.
   ___ e. encourages me.

   Why?

3. The thought of my authority making me my child's servant makes me feel
   ___ a. angry.
   ___ b. selfish.
   ___ c. satisfied.
   ___ d. humble.
   ___ e. successful.

   Why?

4. I feel that my use of authority with my children usually reflects
   ___ a. God as creator.
   ___ b. God as judge.
   ___ c. God as redeemer.
   ___ d. "lording it over."

   Why?

5. To be on equal footing with my children as one redeemed sinner with another makes me feel

____ a. insecure.

____ b. comfortable.

____ c. stripped of power.

____ d. grateful.

____ e. puzzled.

Why?

The Point Is Not Pain

When parents and children relate to each other as redeemed people, the principles of relationships within the church illuminate the biblical understanding of parental authority. Servant authority is the hallmark of church government. Even when that authority is used for discipline, service is the motive. The presentations of church discipline in the New Testament point clearly to the purpose of authority.

Paul explains the process of church discipline in detail in 1 Corinthians 5 and 2 Corinthians 2:5-11. Jesus also outlined the same basic process in Matthew 18:15-20. In contrast to the popular notions of authority and discipline (authoritarian and permissive), the church does not use its disciplinary authority to inflict a penalty or punishment on the offender (for Christ has already been punished for all). Rather the sanction of excommunication is invoked as a last resort, always with the goal of restoring the offender to fellowship and righteousness.

Church discipline, like the law, is one of God's tools to stimulate and direct our growth. The goal of this growth has been expressed a variety of ways in the Bible and throughout church history. Perhaps the expressions most helpful to parents are found in Ephesians 4:12-14 and Philippians 3:7-16. These two passages share several elements and a common thrust with slightly different emphases. The goal is the mature character of Christ. The church is given gifts and authority to help believers grow toward this goal (Eph. 4:11-12). Similarly, parents are given authority so they can help their children grow toward the mature character of Christ.

Defining the mature character of Christ is a lifelong endeavor, as is our growth toward it, a fact that Paul openly acknowledged (Phil. 3:12-13). The church is a community devoted to mutual growth (Eph. 4:15-16). In a similar way, parents should freely express to their children their own need for continuous growth, and should never leave the impression that they are perfect. Parents should also be ready to receive help from their children in a relationship of mutual growth.

Earlier in Philippians, Paul summarized the essential nature of the character of Christ (2:1-11). Christ surrendered the glory of his position as God and gave himself to the humble obedience of the crucifixion. He gave himself in the ultimate service to others (Matt. 20:28; Mark 10:45). In re-

36

sponse, God raised Jesus from the grave and exalted him. As Paul has indicated, Jesus' death and resurrection are the ultimate expressions of the mature character of Christ. His entire lifestyle, as recorded in the gospels, points consistently to this event. Jesus' teachings, as found in the Sermon on the Mount (Matt. 5-7; Luke 6:17-49) and in his parables, clearly teach God's desire for this sort of humble service in his children.

This simplified summary of the mature character of Christ corresponds closely to many of our human understandings of maturity. Maturity is frequently defined as the ability to defer immediate pleasure for a later and greater benefit. Maturity is thinking of others as well as one's self. Maturity is the ability to take responsibility for one's self and, when necessary, for others. Maturity is a healthy, accurate self-image.

Keeping that goal of maturity in mind makes it easier to properly exercise our authority as parents. Parental authority, and the discipline that accompanies it, is often wrongly understood in terms of punishment and making children pay for wrongs they have done. However, Jesus himself already paid for these wrongs with his death. Parental authority, following the pattern of church authority and discipline, should instead stimulate and direct children in their growth toward maturity. The New Testament frequently uses the family to illustrate Christ's intention for the church and vice versa. In fact, family terminology is used in expressing both church discipline and God's direct discipline. Punishment tends to divide and separate (the ultimate punishment is separation from God), while discipline unites, expresses love, and stimulates growth (Prov. 3:12; Heb. 12:6-10; Rev. 3:19).

The family was eating supper when eleven-year-old Mary walked in. Where have you been?" asked Dad with a blend of anger and relief in his voice.

"Over at Sarah's. We just got talking and lost track of time." Sarah hoped a casual answer would defuse what she knew was a touchy situation. She had been late several times recently and had been warned something would have to change. Now she was later than ever.

"Wash up and come to supper. I want some time to think about what to do about you being this late."

After a very quiet supper Dad said, "I have two different ideas about how to keep you from being late. The first is based on my feelings. I get very worried when you're not home on time. I start worrying that you might be hurt or sick or something, and I don't even know where you are. Then when you come in, I'm relieved that you're okay, but I'm angry that you put me through all that anguish. When I feel like that, I want to make you feel a strong enough pain so you come in on time. Maybe I could meet you when school lets out with a sign on the car that says 'Mary must ride home with her Dad so she won't be late.'"

"Oh, Dad, I'd die of embarrassment."

"I know. Part of me wants you to feel that so you know how much I hurt when I worry about you. Another part of me wants you to learn to let me know where you are. I'd like it if you could wear an alarm watch that I could set. A half hour before supper it would go off, and you'd come home automatically."

Mary laughed a little. *"The watch I have now can do that, you know. I could set it for 5:00 P.M. so I'd be home by 5:30."*

"That would be great, if I could just be sure that it would really work. We'd have to decide ahead of time what would happen if you didn't make it. Like, maybe you'd have to miss supper if you didn't make it by the time we started."

"But I'd have trouble doing my homework if I was hungry."

"If you had to go hungry once, you'd be a lot more motivated to get home on time after that."

"That's for sure! But how about this: If I'm late one day, the next day I have to come straight home from school."

"If you mean that, you'll have to come straight home tomorrow."

"But we didn't have that rule until just now."

"But you had been warned that something would happen . . . I'd also be a lot more comfortable in the future if you would let us know when you stop at a friend's house. That way when you call, I can remind you to be sure your alarm is set, too."

"I'll try it for a few days. Can we talk it over again a week from Saturday?"

While love is of utmost importance for conveying servant authority from parent to child, justice is essential if parents' authority is to guide to the mature character of Christ. Building on the work of Lawrence Kohlberg, Ted Ward writes:

> *For Christians the most crucial concern for their families, for their local church congregations and their educational institutions is that they be placed where justice—the high sense of justice inherent in godly righteousness—prevails. There must be respect. There must be dialogue in equity. There must be due process. There must be mercy above retribution. And above all, there must be a concern for God's principles, not as super-laws in the style of the Pharisees, but as transcendent guidance frameworks within which each member works out his or her own transactions with others and defines for himself or herself a continually maturing sense of right and wrong.[1]*

Parents who exert their servant authority establish an environment of justice. They know they are inconsistent in relationships with their children and make no attempt to pretend otherwise. When they have been unjust, such parents confess to the offended child. They also readily forgive when children confess their own injustices. Parents who would seek justice in their families must make themselves vulnerable to their spouses and their children.

Suggestions for Group Session

Opening

As people gather, talk together in small, informal groups about your memories of times you experienced conflicts with someone in authority (parent, teacher or school official, employer or police officer) as children or young people. Share the incidents, feelings, lessons, and memories from these encounters. Writing out these instructions on the chalkboard and pointing them out as people arrive will enable you to get started right away so you do not have a flat, down time before your official session begins.

After a time, gather the whole group together. Share with each other something that you heard in the introductory conversations that you think everyone should hear. Then make sure that everyone has been introduced and has a copy of the book. Before starting group discussion, the leader can open with prayer, asking God to help you understand the truth of the Word and how it applies to your responsibilities as parents.

For Discussion

1. Review the qualities of your children you listed in the Kingdom Catalog on page 27. Embark on a kingdom fantasy voyage with your group by imagining together what God may have in store for your children. Start by talking about how you think God might use them in the service of the kingdom in this age. If you are feeling adventurous, you may go on to speculate what it will be like to be with your children in the fulfilled kingdom.

2. Look over your responses to "Kingdom Construction" on page 30. As a group of parents, discuss with each other what you have been doing that nourishes the growth of kingdom values in your children. In what ways do you think you could be more effective? What insights have you gained from reading and reflecting on this chapter that could help with this process? What possibilities and problems do you see for believing parents who want to guide their children to trust in Jesus?

3. Divide into groups of three, with spouses in different groups. Examine Matthew 20:25-28 or Mark 10:42-45 and John 13:3-17. As a group complete this sentence, "Servant authority is . . ." Write your definition on a sheet of newsprint. After all the groups have written their definitions, they can read the results as they post their sheets around the room with

masking tape. Discuss how these ideas could be practically expressed in parent-child relationships.

4. The concept of servant authority is new, puzzling, or even threatening to many parents. Get in touch with your own feelings by looking over "Your Response to Servant Authority" on pages 35-36. Focus on one item that best reflects your feelings, and talk about it with your group. Concentrate on how you feel at this point, rather than analyzing and evaluating the concept.

5. Tell each other the one most important change that you think the concept of servant authority would make in your relationships with your children if you were more intentionally drawing on it.

6. Form three groups. Each group will write a description of Christlike maturity based on the following Scripture passages.

Group 1	Philippians 2:1-11, Matthew 20:28, Mark 10:45
Group 2	Galatians 5:22-23
Group 3	Matthew 5:3-10

After each group reads its description of Christlike maturity, discuss how these qualities would be evident in children at different ages: preschool, grade-school age, middle school, high school. That is, what does it mean to be Christlike and appropriately mature at any particular age, say five or nine or thirteen or seventeen? (Save these descriptions for a more in-depth discussion of Christlike maturity in session five.)

7. Compare and contrast the use of discipline for punishment and for growth. A way to do this is to use two newsprint pads or a divided chalkboard. Title one side "Discipline for Punishment" and the other "Discipline for Growth." List contrasting qualities across from each other. As you develop this listing, talk about how these two approaches to discipline relate to specific occasions for discipline in your families.

8. Identify the mechanisms of working out justice in your families. In what ways do you think parents and children in your families see justice similarly and differently? In what ways do you think your children's experience of justice in your families influences their spiritual development?

Closing

By this second session the makeup of the group should be fairly well established. People should be getting comfortable with each other and building group trust. Make the most of this by setting up prayer partnerships for the remainder of the course.

Each of you should write your name and phone number on a 3" x 5" card. Then take turns describing one concern you have about your relationship with your children for which you would appreciate some prayer support.

Find a partner you feel free to talk to about your problem in greater detail. Then exchange cards and promise to support each other through prayer and conversation in the weeks to come. Pray briefly for each other before the group is dismissed.

Carry your partner's card with you for the duration of the course and make a point to pray for your partner at least once each week. You might even want to contact each other privately once in a while for updates and encouragement.

THREE

PORTABLE, PERMANENT RESPONSIBILITY

Twelve-year-old Jason had been saving money from his paper route to buy a bike. He had about $125. But after spending the afternoon with one of his friends who had a stereo in his room, Jason took his money and bought an inexpensive stereo at the local discount store.

He was happy with the new-found popularity this purchase brought him for a couple of weeks. But one afternoon, as friends were rough-housing in his room, the stereo fell to the floor, and the door to the CD player cracked in half. Jason angrily sent his friends home. Disappointed, he sulked in his room until his dad came home from work.

"Dad, I never should have bought that stupid stereo! It's busted, and I don't have any more money to buy the bike I wanted. I sure am stupid, blowing the money for the bike on that stereo. It will take me three months just to get back where I was—and that's if I work every chance I can get. I won't be able to buy the bike until summer is over."

How should Jason's dad respond? Should he scold Jason for his irresponsibility? Should he try to console Jason? Should he come up with the cash to help Jason get the bike on schedule (an especially tempting option if Dad shared the joy of anticipating a new bike this summer with his son)? Parents have considerable power at their disposal at times such as these. The way Jason's dad uses that power will have a significant affect on Jason.

In this situation, as in most that involve parental decision-making, Dad has the opportunity to use his authority to serve his son. Though Dad has his own strong feelings right now, Jason is the one with the problem. By listening attentively and helping Jason get in touch with the problem and the way he feels about it, Dad can give Jason the opportunity to take responsibility for his own behavior.

Jason may be on the threshold of a new level of maturity, and having to wait the full time for the new bike (and having to do without it for the summer) may be the stimulus he needs for this growth. On the other hand, Jason may not be mature enough yet to deal with such disappointment. If that seems to be the case, Dad will have to try a modified approach. Dad knows that just giving Jason the money so that he can buy the bike on schedule will not build his maturity and responsibility. However, Dad may feel that he made a mistake in permitting Jason to take charge of such a large amount of money in the first place. Jason just wasn't mature enough for that much responsibility. So in the interest of justice (and mercy), Dad and Jason may work out another arrangement. It might include delaying the purchase of the bike, but not the full time. It might include a loan to be paid in cash and chores. It might include new arrangements for holding Jason's money, such as a savings account with Dad's name on it in trust for Jason.

By helping Jason with these decisions, Dad can use his authority to serve his son so he will grow as much as possible through this experience.

Responsibility for Responsibility

Parents have the responsibility to build responsibility in their children. When children are very young, they are dependent on parents for everything, and parents make all the necessary decisions. If parents do not exercise complete authority in their care for a newborn baby, the child will die. As children grow, they are allowed increasing freedom to make their own decisions (and to learn to live with the consequences), until they are ready for the independence of adulthood.

Because of the authority delegated to them, parents determine which decisions their children are ready to make on their own. Our goal as parents should be to allow our children to make as many decisions for themselves as they are ready to take responsibility for (by honestly facing the consequences).

The different levels of responsibility become quite apparent in our home in what we expect of our six-year-old and our seventeen-year-old. In the area of homework, for example, the difference in pronounced.

In first grade, Erik is just being introduced to the routines of assignments and deadlines. He needs to know that we will ask for a list of assignments every day, and that we will look at any work that is to be turned in. We need to set aside time each evening for him to do homework. It is our responsibility to establish a balanced schedule of play, reading, television, homework, and organized activities such as sports.

As a high school senior, David, on the other hand, is ready for a lot more independence. He still needs our encouragement and occasional nudging, but he is responsible for tracking his own assignments and setting his own study schedule. He must determine the level of performance that is acceptable. Even if we as parents wanted to, imposing and enforcing our standards would be impossible. We must trust that these sorts of things were established in the patterns of earlier years. What David needs from us now is affirmation, encouragement, and support. He needs to know that we are available to help at his request.

Finding the right match and balance for each child is not always easy. At times, Erik needs permission to strike out on his own with the confidence that we will stand ready to protect him from disaster and to celebrate a new triumph. That may happen, for example, the first time he studies for a spelling test without drill and review with Mom or Dad. At times, David needs to be reminded to give a project his best rather than just getting by. Such a nudge might be appropriate, for example, when he's working on a short history paper that counts for very few points but could make a stellar impression because it is on a well-liked and familiar topic.

Though parents, as authorities, are in charge of this process of deciding how much responsibility is appropriate at each age, they should involve their children in their decisions. This involvement takes two main forms. First, children should be involved in determining what decisions they will make, so that they can be exposed to the justice of that determination. Second, they should be expected to follow through on their own decisions. They may ask for help, but parents should avoid meddling once the decision has been made—unless disastrous results are imminent (recall, for example, the story of Janet and her mother in chapter 2).

When building responsibility in this way, parents will find that it's very important not to rescue their children from the consequences of bad decisions. In fact, some of the most valuable learning experiences come from suffering the consequences of bad decisions when we are young—and when the consequences are of minor and brief duration. In this way the pattern (and the value of parental perspective) can be learned before battles erupt over life-changing decisions that come at an ever-increasing pace from adolescence on. As hard as it is for parents to watch their children suffer, this is a necessary part of building responsibility.

Parents can use their authority to cultivate responsibility by building in some consequences to actions they are particularly concerned about.

Getting everyone to dinner on time in the summer has always been a challenge for us. The boys want to squeeze every drop of fun out of the daylight. After a few weeks of frustration one summer, we negotiated a new procedure. We bought a large cow bell, and my wife and I accepted the responsibility for ringing it five minutes before suppertime each night. We assigned the boys the responsibility of either being within earshot of the bell or letting us know where they were so that we could notify them by telephone of the impending meal. And we clearly outlined the consequences for not living up to this responsibility: Anyone who was not at the table by the time the others were eating had to wait until breakfast for his next meal.

On one occasion we rang the bell vigorously, but Jon did not appear. We slowed the serving process, but he still did not show up. Finally, the family sat down to eat at the picnic table in the backyard. When we were almost finished, Jon rounded the corner and observed the situation. As he passed the table, he said, "I know—no supper. Nothing until breakfast." With that, he went into the house, cleaned up for bed, and never said another word about it. He ate ravenously at breakfast and didn't miss another supper all summer!

It hasn't always gone that smoothly. Though I think our dinner-on-time system is a good strategy, it's not without its moments of stress (on a couple of occasions, a very hungry boy has awakened in the middle of the night and been given a small mercy snack to carry him though to breakfast). But though I have felt the anguish of depriving my children of three or four meals in their lifetimes, I am confident they have not suffered nutritionally or emotionally. This has been one strategy in building a whole pattern of responsible family communication and scheduling.

Keeping Pace

Matching the level of responsibility with a child's maturity is not easy for parents. Expecting too much too soon strains a child's ability to cope with life. Not expecting enough will stunt development. Restlessness and minor apparent irresponsibility are often cues that the child is ready for bigger responsibility. Frustration and a sense of helplessness may be signs that parents are expecting too much.

The first day of school is a great time to take note of children moving to new levels of responsibility. Preschoolers and kindergartners are tentative and tingling with excitement. They are learning the routines of crossing the street to school or taking the bus on their own. For many, this is the first extended time away from home without their parents and the first experience with structured group time.

First grade signals the first full year of grade school. For many children the first few weeks are a difficult transition into a longer, more structured routine. They learn that they are going to have to build their endurance.

By the time they head off to middle school, children often want to give up the new clothes and equipment that signal inexperience. They want to appear seasoned and familiar with the routines. With some fear they face the new challenges of locker combinations, changing classes, dressing for gym, a mounting homework load, and the impending specter of adolescence. The end of the school day throbs with social interaction. "Who do you have for English?" "I can hardly believe they gave me gym first period."

46

Children of this age are more likely to gather with friends than return directly home.

High school students mix bravado with feigned boredom. The new freshmen, who seemed so grown-up at last June's eighth-grade graduation program, are dwarfed by the externally adult seniors. Some of the older students drive to school—nothing enhances a high school student's status as much as driving or being invited to ride. The halting crushes of early adolescence bloom into the romances of steady couples who find some way to arrive at school together the first day, even from clear across town. The seniors know this year is it. While they have been longing to be grown-up for eighteen years, they may shudder at the prospects of college, career, military, marriage. They grasp for freedom and hope responsibility doesn't bind too tightly.

Think of your own children. Are they ready for new, more significant responsibilities? Are they over their heads in any areas? In the spaces below, write in a sentence or two about the next step of responsibility that you feel each of your children will be ready for. This should include a description of how you, as a parent, will encourage this step of growth. Also note any evidence you can to explain why you feel this is the most appropriate next step.

1. Name of child:
   Next step of responsibility:

   How you will encourage this growth:

   Evidence that this is the next stage:

2. Name of child:
   Next step of responsibility:

   How you will encourage this growth:

   Evidence that this is the next stage:

3. Name of child:
   Next step of responsibility:

   How you will encourage this growth:

   Evidence that this is the next stage:

4. Name of child:
   Next step of responsibility:

   How you will encourage this growth:

   Evidence that this is the next stage:

5. Name of child:
   Next step of responsibility:

   How you will encourage this growth:

   Evidence that this is the next stage:

6. Name of child:
   Next step of responsibility:

   How you will encourage this growth:

   Evidence that this is the next stage:

Talking and Listening with Skill

While teaching the skills of effective parenting is beyond the scope of this book, it is nevertheless good to recognize that certain skills are potent tools for exercising the principles of servant authority. Two of these basic skills are *active listening* and *"I" messages*. We will look at each of these skills briefly in the pages that follow. You can learn more about these skills and how to use them in both secular and Christian parent-training programs. When built on or evaluated against a solid biblical base, such training courses can be of great value to Christian parents who intend to use their authority as servants of their children.

The first skill, active listening, is the process by which parents verbally reflect to a child the feelings the child is expressing. ("You feel put down when your friends spread rumors about you.") This helps both parents and children gain an understanding of the situation and the emotions evoked by it. It helps children accept ownership of their own emotions and problems. It helps children assume responsibility for solving their own problems and making their own decisions. Active listening is one thing parents can do to help equip their children to direct their own lives.

To get an idea of how active listening responses are formed, study the list below. Then try writing your own active listening responses.

1. Mom, I'm never going to let that careless, clumsy Carolyn use any of my things again.
   Response: You're angry that she broke your necklace.

2. Look at this English paper! I've never gotten an A from Mr. Abbott before. He's the toughest teacher in the school.
   Response: You're pleased and proud that you did so well on that paper. You're sure that means you're doing really good work.

3. What a stupid test! I can't believe she gave me a D. If I hadn't thought I knew that stuff, I wouldn't have gone to the movie last night.
   Response: You're disappointed that you didn't do better on the test and angry at yourself for not studying more.

4. Hey! Was that ever a great youth group party! We laughed so hard I couldn't believe it. And you should have seen the boy I met. He was so nice.
   Response: You're happy with how much you enjoy your friends and excited about meeting a new boy.

5. I don't want to come in and go to bed. I want to play with my friends. It's still light out.
   Response: You're having a good time, and you are disappointed you have to quit.

Now try your hand at writing some active listening responses.

6. This stupid toy is so cheap that it broke. I hate it!
   Response:

7. Come quick! Look at my garden! I got all the weeds out and you can see new little flowers on the forget-me-nots.
   Response:

8. I want that Ninja Turtle toy. Buy it for me. Buy it! Buy it!
   Response:

9. I won! I won! Meet the new student council president.
   Response:

10. Be quiet! I can't concentrate on my homework with Dad's power saw running in the basement. It's giving me a headache. I deserve some respect too.
    Response:

When You Need Them to Listen to You

Using "I" messages is a technique by which parents can confront children with the effects of their behavior without degrading or "lording it over" them. In an "I" message, parents express their own feelings, identify the behavior of the child that provoked these feelings, and explain why the behavior bothers or pleases them. ("I feel taken advantage of when you leave your clothes and school books on the entryway floor, because I have to move them to your room or stumble over them until you leave for school in the morning.")

The process of formulating an "I" message allows parents to own their own feelings and clearly identify what is disturbing them. The "I" message lets children know how their behavior is affecting their parents. It encourages them to alter their behavior out of consideration and respect for the parent. Generally, it helps children develop more respectful, responsible relationships with other people. "I" messages are most appropriate when the emotions, and the problem that provoked them, belong to the parent.

"I" messages have three parts. Part one is "I feel . . ." in which the parent describes his or her primary emotional response to the specific situation. Part two is "when . . ." in which the parent describes the particular behavior that elicits these emotions. Part three is "because . . ." in which the parent explains how this behavior affects him or her. Look at these examples to see how "I" messages are constructed.

1. *I feel* angry *when* you forget to feed and clean up after the dog, *because* you promised me that if we got a pet, you would be responsible for looking after it.

2. *I feel* a deep satisfaction *when* I see you singing with your friends in worship, *because* I feel my efforts at teaching you about God and including you in the church have been worthwhile.

3. *I feel* anxious *when* you go to a friend's house after school without checking in with me first, *because* I don't know if you are okay or how to get in touch with you.

4. *I feel* warm and comfortable *when* we play games as a family, *because* I have a lot of fun being with you.

5. *I feel* hurt *when* you don't want to share your homework with me, *because* I think I could really help, especially with history and English.

Now try writing your own "I" messages by filling in the blanks for these situations.

6. *Situation:* Teenager returns from a Friday night outing with friends nearly an hour past the agreed-upon deadline.

   I feel
   when
   because

7. *Situation:* You observe your child defending a handicapped child in the neighborhood from the teasing of a group of thoughtless children.

I feel
when
because

8. *Situation:* You are working on paying the monthly bills and balancing the checkbook. A group of noisy children are playing in your yard and seem to be squabbling a lot. Just when you've had about all you can take, you hear your child's voice above all the others: "Let's have a screaming contest."

I feel
when
because

9. *Situation:* Your children got together to plan a surprise eighteenth wedding anniversary party for you. After the celebration supper you are helping them with the final details of clean-up.

I feel
when
because

10. *Situation:* You are getting tired of shutting the door to hide your child's messy room. You have not washed his underwear for over two weeks, and you know he must be reusing dirty clothes from the heap in the middle of the room. When you see the new jacket he begged for for his birthday seeping out from under the pile and tangled around the desk leg, you feel you have reached your limit.

I feel
when
because

Better Than the Best Solution You Can Offer

Sometimes when children have a problem, parents are tempted to propose solutions to the problem rather than helping the child deal with his or her emotions. For example, telling a child who has been the victim of vicious gossip to ignore it and find some new friends does not take into account the hurt that has been inflicted. The offered "solution" only adds to the child's sense of inadequacy.

On the other hand, sometimes when parents have a problem with something their children have done or left undone, such as leaving a messy pile of magazines and CD's by the stereo in the living room, they act as though it is the child's problem. Actually, of course, the child has no problem with the mess; it is the parents who are bothered and want to bring about a change.

The story has been told many ways, often as a joke that brings a knowing smile to children and a painful grimace to parents: The family goes to a restaurant, and the children's menu offers chicken, a hot dog, a hamburger, or a grilled cheese. When the waitress comes to take the family's order, Mother says, "She'll have the chicken." At the same time the child says, "I want a hot dog!"

"And what would you like to drink with your hot dog?" asks the waitress.

"She'll have milk," says Mother. "Apple juice," pipes up the child simultaneously.

"I'll bring your apple juice with your hot dog," says the waitress.

As the waitress walks away from the table, the child says, "She thinks I'm a real person."

Whether the waitress's responsibility is really to the child or to the parents is a legitimate social and business question. Nevertheless, even very young children appreciate being included in decisions that affect them. While parents may rightly be concerned about nutrition, it's reasonable for a child to care about enjoying a meal. The child's perception of being treated as a "real person" is more important than the menu selection. By talking with the child about the choice before the waitress took the order, Mother might well have convinced the child to order chicken and milk. Certainly Mother could have avoided an awkward situation that may have contributed to her child's feelings of inadequacy. Imposing a solution or decision on others as though they are incapable of participating in their own lives is demeaning and oppressive.

Diagnosis and Prescription

Active listening and "I" messages are powerful tools for parents to use to serve their children. But determining when to use which one can be difficult, especially in the midst of an emotionally charged situation. The basic question to ask is, who has the problem? Whoever has the problem needs someone to listen to them. Thus, when parents detect that children have problems, they can use active listening. On the other hand, when parents own the problems, they can use "I" messages to get their children to listen.

This may sound simple enough, but in practice the application is not so obvious. Sometimes it may seem that the one whose behavior has provoked the problem is the one who owns the problem, but he or she may not see it that way. For example, who owns the problem when Mom and Dad are waiting at 2 A.M. for Susan, who has missed a midnight deadline for returning from a date? While it may seem that the daughter has the problem since she is the one who is late, she may come bouncing in the door, bubbling over with the excitement of her romantic adventure. It's Mom and Dad who have the problem—their anxiety and anger is mixed with the relief of seeing their daughter arrive home safely. Because they want Susan to hear their concern, they can use an "I" message something like this: "I'm so relieved to see you home. I felt fearful and angry when you didn't come home or call, because I couldn't find out where you were or if you were all right."

At other times parents take on problems that really belong to their children. For example, Mom is fixing supper on an early summer evening. Several neighborhood children are playing in the yard. She starts to listen when the conversation gets loud and is punctuated with shouts of "That's not fair!" "No, it's my turn first!" and "I called it first! I'm the boss." Then she hears her son Jimmy: "This is my house. You all have to go home!" The door slams and Jimmy stomps to his bedroom. At this point, Mom may be tempted to tell Jimmy to be nice to his friends and go back out and apologize. Such an approach discounts the reality of Jimmy's feelings and demeans his integrity by judgmentally assuming he is at fault. Active listening is a better approach to serving Jimmy's needs: "You feel frustrated when your friends argue over playing fair."

One way of determining who owns the problem is to ask yourself who is experiencing the feelings. Who is expressing their emotions verbally or nonverbally? Rather than telling a tearful child, "It's all right. You can stop crying," let the child know you will listen to his feelings by saying "You're upset by something." And instead of attacking a child with, "You're inconsiderate and irresponsible," an angry parent will be more effective by saying, "I feel angry and frustrated when you don't cut the grass on schedule, because then I have to squeeze it into my list if I want it to look good for the weekend."

The biblical concept of law and gospel offers another way of determining who owns the problem, a way that is fundamentally rooted in the biblical concept of servant authority. In his book *You Can Have a Family Where Everybody Wins*, Earl Gaulke expresses well the appropriate use of both law and gospel in the family.

> *The Law teaches us what we are to do and not to do; the Gospel teaches us what God has done. The Law is to be preached to impenitent sinners (including the "flesh" of Christians); the Gospel to those who are troubled and alarmed because of their sins. . . . While the Law is a guide to Christian behavior, . . . only the Gospel . . . can really change and power the Christian person to do what the Law requires.[1]*

The message of Romans and Galatians calls all Christians to live by grace. It encourages parents to relate their authority to their children through the gospel, while the use of law should stimulate a desire for the gospel. Examine these focal passages to deepen your understanding of the underlying New Testament teaching about law and gospel. Read Romans 6:14-7:25 and Galatians 3:1-4:31 and fill in the following compare-and-contrast chart. Though this is a substantial amount of material to study, it is pivotal to the whole message of God's grace and the theological foundation for the redemptive use of parental authority.

What similarities and parallels can you identify between law and gospel?

	Romans 6-7	Galatians 3-4
Law		
Gospel		

What differences and contrasts can you identify between law and gospel?

	Romans 6-7	Galatians 3-4
Law		
Gospel		

While the concepts of law and gospel are deeply rooted in the biblical message, they are much more than the hidden structure behind the scenes. The way Christians understand these concepts has profound implications for the way they live their faith in relationship with other people. Law and gospel suggest practical strategies for parents in knowing how to respond to specific situations with their children. From such thinking, parents can learn to serve their children by cultivating a grasp of God's righteous expectations and his loving mercy.

Nine-year-old Jane comes to Mother on the verge of tears. "I spilled my juice while I was watching TV. I'm sorry, Mom, I wasn't being careful enough."

Now is not the time for a scolding or for confronting Jane about her frequent carelessness. Jane already recognizes her responsibility. The gospel is the tool Mother's authority uses here. Active listening is an appropriate response. The subsequent conversation might go something like this:

"You're afraid I'm going to be angry with you for spilling your juice," Mother responds to Jane's confession.

"Well, yes. But I guess have it coming."

"You really feel bad about the spilled juice. You think I have a good reason to be upset."

"Yeah. I mean, it's such a mess, and the rug will have to be washed."

"You're sorry for the extra work cleaning up makes for me."

"Uh huh. Will you forgive me?"

"Of course."

"Can I help clean up?"

"Yes, go get the bucket and brush in the basement."

Now imagine the situation is changed slightly. Instead of Jane coming to Mother about the spilled juice, Mother discovers the juice on the rug and Jane watching TV with complete disinterest. In this instance Jane has made no effort to accept responsibility for her action. She needs a confrontation with the (gracious) law. An "I" message is an appropriate way for Mother to express her servant authority. The conversation may go something like this:

> *"Jane, I'm upset that your juice is spilled because I will have to wash the rug now."*
>
> *"Aw, Mom!"*
>
> *"And I'm disappointed that you didn't tell me about it right away, because it will be harder to get out now."*
>
> *"But I was watching TV."*
>
> *"I feel taken advantage of when you choose to watch TV instead of cleaning up your spill, because it leaves me with the mess."*
>
> *"Oh, Mom, I'm sorry. I just wasn't thinking. I guess I figured you'd clean it up . . ."*
>
> *"I feel I am treated unfairly when you leave a mess for me to clean up without making an effort to help."*
>
> *"I thought maybe it wasn't so bad, and no one would notice."*
>
> *"Well it can't be ignored. It will get sticky and leave a stain if we don't clean it. I feel bad when I get stuck cleaning up messes I didn't make."*
>
> *"O.K., can I do something to help?"*
>
> *"Sure, get the bucket and brush in the basement."*
>
> *"And, Mom, will you forgive me?"*
>
> *"Of course."*

Naturally children will not always respond as rapidly or as positively as the child in these examples. Also, once the child receives Mother's "I" message, the child may have a problem and need to be listened to actively. But despite all the variations that may arise in a live situation, Jane's spilled juice does illustrate how thinking in terms of law and gospel can guide parents in using active listening and "I" messages. When the child recognizes responsibility (confession) and expresses a desire to change (repentance), the gospel is appropriate. The parent may use active listening to serve the child, and the child can express emotions and decide on a responsible course of action.

On the other hand, when the child refuses to acknowledge irresponsible behavior and makes no effort to restore the relationship, the law is appropriate. The parent may then confront the child with an "I" message. This serves to confront the child with the results of his or her actions and encourages a responsible decision.

Look at the following situations and decide whether you think law or gospel is most appropriate. Also decide what the parent's first response might be.

1. Katie comes to dinner and says, "Dad, I really blew my science test. I know I turned down your help. After supper could we review? Then maybe you could call Mrs. Hubbard and see if she'd let me have a retest."

_____ Law

_____ Gospel

Response:

2. Daniel's counselor has phoned to ask for a parents' conference. She says that he has not turned in any homework for over two weeks and has a couple of unexcused absences as well.

_____ Law

_____ Gospel

Response:

3. The Andersons are on a rotating schedule for mowing the lawn. Each of their three teenage children take turns. They have developed a check list of the tasks that must be done by Saturday each week: mow, rake, edge, etc. This week it was Cathy's turn. She cut the grass on Saturday, but as the Andersons back out of the driveway to meet friends for dinner on Saturday night, they see evidence of sloppy work: piles of clippings have been left in the corners, the edges are shaggy, and the mower was left outside the shed.

_____ Law

_____ Gospel

Response:

4. The Johnstone family is on vacation. They have about a ten- hour drive to the lake cabin they have rented. Mr. and Mrs. Johnstone were up until 3:00 A.M. packing the car. They left at 8:00 A.M., very tired. The children, ten-year-old Jenny and seven-year-old Jeff, were quiet and sleepy all morning, but after a picnic lunch, they become more alert and irritable. Mr. and Mrs. Johnstone have switched off driving and sleeping. By 2 P.M. the parents can no longer sleep, but not because they're rested. Jenny and Jeff have been playing a license plate game. The tension erupts into a fight when Jeff screams, "I saw that Hawaii license plate first. Mom, make her give me the points."

_____ Law

_____ Gospel

Response:

5. Seventeen-year-old Mike crept into the house after 1 A.M., hoping his parents would have gone to bed. As he stepped into the living room, the light went on, and his father sat up on the couch. "Where have you been this late?" Dad asked with undisguised anger. Mike answered with a quiver in his voice, "I've been sitting in the car in the driveway thinking since 11:30. Julie broke up with me after the concert tonight."

_____ Law

_____ Gospel

Response:

Think back over the last month. Identify a situation for each of your children in which he or she needed the law and one in which he or she needed the gospel. Use just a phrase to describe the situation in these spaces.

Name of Child:
Law Situation:

Gospel Situation:

Name of Child:
Law Situation:

Gospel Situation:

Name of Child:
Law Situation:

Gospel Situation:

Name of Child:
Law Situation:

Gospel Situation:

Name of Child:
Law Situation:

Gospel Situation:

Name of Child:
Law Situation:

Gospel Situation:

Parents can also use active listening and "I" messages to serve their children in positive situations. Servant authority is not limited to situations of conflict and irresponsibility.

For example, active listening can be used to build the child's sense of accomplishment and self-esteem.

Five-year-old Darrell comes home from school and announces, "Mom, I tied my own shoelaces and put on my own boots at school today. All by myself!"

"You're proud of being able to take care of your own shoes and boots now."

"I sure am. Now I don't have to wait for the teacher."

"You're really happy you can be more on your own and don't have to depend on the teacher so much. You feel more grown up now."

"Sure do!"

Parents can also use "I" messages to build their children's sense of worth. This is particularly reflective of servant authority in that the parent takes the initiative. A few examples illustrate this point.

"You know, Jim, I felt very proud to be your father when I saw you help Mrs. Smith carry in her groceries. I think helping and being considerate of other people is important."

"Ann, I was pleasantly surprised to come home from shopping and find the dishes all washed. I was afraid I wouldn't have time to do them before supper."

"I'm really excited that you made the football team, Dirk, because it's something you've looked forward to for a long time, and I want you to enjoy it."

"I'm glad you got an 'A' on that English paper because you worked so hard on it, and I'm pleased all the work paid off for you."

"I sure enjoyed playing games with you kids tonight. It's one of my favorite ways to spend an evening."

Building Children

One of the most significant services parents can provide is an environment in which their children can grow into mature, responsible adults. In fact, parents have authority from God for this specific purpose. Active listening and "I" messages are two tools parents can use to serve their children, but they are not enough. Parents also need strategies for handling tough situations with sensitivity. They need a plan for communicating their values effectively to their children. In facing these needs, the use of servant authority becomes intensely practical.

Suggestions for Group Session

Opening

Have a large sheet of butcher paper taped on a wall and make some markers available. (You may want to use a double thickness of the paper to prevent marker bleed-through to the wall.) Put this statement in large letters at the top of the paper:

"I remember when my parent(s) opened up to me . . ."

As people arrive, they can write completions to that statement on the paper. These may be memories of experiences or reactions to memories. Group members may respond to each other's comments in writing or in conversation with each other.

Once everyone has arrived, gather as a group. Begin by discussing when you think you were first aware of your parents' emotional vulnerability. In what situation and in what way, if ever, did your parent(s) first let you in on their own personal needs? What was your reaction as child, young person, or adult?

Then spend several minutes praying as a group about your parents. These may be expressions of thanks for what parents contributed to you or prayers for their current needs.

For Discussion

1. Gather in subgroups, with parents whose children are of similar ages meeting together. Compare notes with each other to identify the central issues in your children's current stage of development. What are the topics that seem to be shared by many parents? What individual differences come up? You may want to look at the "Next Steps of Responsibility" exercise on pages 47-48 to assist you in contributing to this discussion.

   Continue your discussion by sharing strategies that have seemed helpful in encouraging your children to develop their maturity. You may wish to take notes on helpful insights you gain from other parents.

2. Review the technique of active listening. Form triads for practicing this skill. One person will take the role of a child and may choose from the examples and exercises on page 49 to start the conversation. A second person will take the role of the parent, who will use the active listening skill. The third person will be an observer who will not participate in the conversation but will listen carefully to the interaction of the other two, paying special attention to the use of active listening skills. The idea is to continue the conversation for several interchanges to get a feel for what happens when parents use active listening.

   After the conversation, the observer should tell the other two what he or she heard. Then change roles. The observer becomes the parent; the parent becomes the child; the child becomes the observer. Repeat the rotation a third time so that each person has taken all three roles. If time allows, spend a few minutes with the whole group, talking about what you have just learned about using active listening effectively.

3. Review the technique of "I" messages. Use the same triads described in the previous activity. In this case, the one taking the parent role chooses the starting situation from the exercise on pages 50-51.

Again, encourage each member of each triad to try all three roles.

4. As a group of parents, share with each other authority situations you have faced recently with your children. As each parent describes a situation, the group should suggest whether active listening or "I" messages seem the more appropriate strategy to use. Without getting into a debate, talk about reasons for the selection. The idea is to sharpen diagnostic skills rather than defend a particular selection. Also, talk a little about how the use of that particular skill might affect the situation.

5. Divide into four groups. Designate one group to look at Romans 6-7 for information about the law, and a second group for information about the gospel. A third group will look at Galatians 3-4 to gather data about the law, and a fourth group will focus on the gospel in the Galatians passage. Of course, these groups may draw on what they wrote in the charts on page 54. Each group should designate a recorder/reporter who will take notes on sheets of newsprint and prepare to report to the whole class. As the groups report, assemble the sheets of newsprint to resemble the chart on page 54. You may add further insights to the chart in your book if you wish.

6. As a group, discuss ways that using the concepts of law and gospel can help you figure out how to use your parental authority to serve your children effectively. Reviewing your responses to the exercise on pages 56-57 will help start the discussion. Once underway, shift the emphasis to your own children, as you did on page 57. As you wrap up this discussion, try to formulate some principles for using law and gospel to exercise servant authority as parents.

7. Brainstorm together ways in which you could use active listening and "I" messages to build characteristics of maturity in your children. Designate one person to record the ideas on newsprint sheets posted where all can see. Suggest ideas as quickly as they can be recorded. Do not elaborate the details or evaluate the quality of the ideas; one idea may suggest another. If someone will agree to type and duplicate the list, it will be a helpful take-home tool for parents.

Closing

Remember the opening activity in which you talked about your youthful perceptions of your parents and prayed for them. Think ahead and imagine your children discussing the same issues when they are grown. If they could speak from the perspective of that anticipated maturity, what do you think they would want you to do now? Conclude your class by praying for each other, asking God to enable you to be the kind of parents your children need.

¹Gaulke, Earl. *You Can Have a Family Where Everybody Wins*. St. Louis, MO: Concordia Press, 1975, page 24.

SESSION FOUR

DON'T ACCEPT A CHEAP COUNTERFEIT

When I hear all the voices directed to me as a parent, I feel like I am tiptoeing along a razor-thin ridge between two slippery slopes. One set of voices warns me of the dangers of not keeping my children under control with close structure and strict discipline. The pressure can be like a buffeting wind that threatens to push me over the edge and put my pride ahead of my relationship with my children. Other voices caution me about the damage that can be caused by being overbearing, rigid, and untrusting. Their blast pushes me toward a slide into permissiveness, crushing me and my children with insecurity.

Sometimes these forces seem to be swirling whirlwinds, upsetting my precarious balance. They provoke fearful overreaction that could lead to opposing disasters. More often, though, they come as subtle whispers, like sirens luring unsuspecting sailors to shipwreck on rocky shoals. What starts out as confrontation becomes judgment. What passes for freedom is really unbridled license. What could have been constructive discipline is instead punishment that leaves only pain in its wake.

Confrontation or Judgment?

The New Testament warns believers not to judge one another (Matt. 7:1; Rom. 14:13) and even seems to suggest that the judging of nonbelievers be left exclusively to God (Rom. 12:19-21; 1 Cor. 5:12-13). From the usual human understanding, these passages seem to be in conflict with much of what Scripture says about authority and church discipline. However, that's only because we tend to connect judgment and discipline.

63

Matthew 18 and 1 Corinthians 5-6 give explicit instructions for church discipline. These passages can serve as models for the way parents should exercise necessary disciplinary authority *without judging* their children.

The objective of church discipline is to bring about reconciliation with as little embarrassment for both the church and the individual as possible (2 Cor. 2). The clearly outlined steps of this disciplinary procedure always involve direct confrontation, which gives the accused the opportunity to explain or contradict the accusation. Only after church rulers have followed the specified steps of discipline are they permitted to take action, and even then, not to punish the accused but to try to lovingly restore him or her to the church fellowship.

Parents who exercise servant authority will use a similar kind of discipline with their children. Confrontation (sometimes expressed in an "I" message) helps parents avoid the trap of judgment, which is unbiblical and usually resisted by children. Confrontation admits the possibility that the parent might be wrong, and allows the child to act in response to the expressed needs of the parents, rather than reacting to the parent's accusation. Because confrontation is built on love, it avoids the attitudes and feelings of attack and put-down that invariably accompany judgment, and it seeks the restoration of the relationship. Confrontation allows parents to express their own emotions, needs, and desires (thus it is not permissive) while at the same time allowing for due process and responsible action (thus it is not authoritarian).

Julie's Dress

Mother has just found the new dress Julie is to wear for high school graduation stuffed under Julie's bed along with an assortment of other dirty clothes. Although Julie has improved considerably in remembering that Mom has asked her to put dirty clothes down the clothes chute, Mom still checks under the bed on wash days. She hasn't found anything there for several weeks, but today she finds quite a pile. Julie and Mom have worked out an agreement on these dirty clothes, but the new graduation dress is another matter.

Mom is now faced with a choice. Will she judge Julie or confront her? Imagine you are Julie's mother, and write down the first sentence you would say to your daughter when she returns from school.

If you were Julie, how would you feel if you heard your mother say this to you?

Why?

Does your statement seem to reflect a positive confrontation or a judgmental put-down?

Why?

How can you rework your statement to make it a more positive and powerful confrontation and minimize the spirit of judgment?

How about the following approach:

"Julie, I was disappointed to find your new graduation dress with some dirty clothes under your bed. I want your dress to stay nice for graduation next week, and I don't want to have to have it dry-cleaned at the last minute."

If you were Julie, how would you feel if you heard your mother say this to you?

Why?

What might you say in response to your mother?

How would you predict a conversation started this way would end?

Submission or Obedience?

Acts 14 and 15 make a distinction between submission and obedience. In this passage, a debate arose over whether it was proper for Gentiles to be church members without submitting to Jewish customs. In this matter, the disciples specifically told the church leaders that they would have to decide for themselves what they thought was right before God. The disciples continued to preach and accepted the consequences. Through this process, they submitted to the church leaders' authority, even though they did not obey. The difference is subtle, but it has a profound effect on how one responds in an authority conflict.

Proper obedience is a positive biblical concept. To be sure, God expects obedience to his righteous commands. In the Old Testament, children who persistently disobeyed their parents were stoned to death (Deut. 21:18-21). In the New Testament, children are instructed to obey their parents in the Lord (Eph. 6:1). However, this kind of obedience is nothing like the illegitimate demands of unquestioning obedience that some parents make. Instead, it is a consistent and loving expression of the need for submission.

When properly exercised, parental authority produces respect without demanding unquestioning obedience. Thus, in exercising biblical authority, parents respect the child's right to disagree, to have a different opinion, and even to choose a different course of action. This sort of authority is used with the awareness that underlying attitudes are more significant than specific conduct—though they are related, of course. Parents who expect submission can be open to exploring differences of opinion with their children without having their authority threatened. Parents who demand unquestioning obedience, on the other hand, may get temporary, outward conformity, while breeding a rebellious spirit in their children.

This aspect of exercising biblical authority is perhaps the hardest for parents to accept. It seems almost directly opposite to authority, and it places the high risk of parenthood in stark reality. Parents must allow their children the freedom to disobey. Only if the child is free to disobey (and accept the consequences of that choice) is the child's obedience meaningful and authentic. To grant a child this freedom, the parent must recognize the child as a separate person who is responsible to God. This is not to say that parents should do nothing to influence their children or to protect them from imminent danger. Rather, parents must seek to build in their children a sense of personal responsibility to God.

Parents who do not allow this freedom to choose the wrong often discover that their children conform to their wishes only when the threat of punishment is present. In many such families, children openly rebel in later years. If the child's new nature is not allowed to exercise and grow strong while young, the old nature takes over when the external restraints of authoritarian parents are removed or become ineffective.

John and Betty were both raised in very strict families, and their parents instilled in them very high standards of Christian behavior. Since they never challenged those standards as they were growing up, they didn't expect their children to challenge them either. However, as their children entered high school, they began questioning John and Betty's rules. They discovered that other Christian families did not insist on these same rigid standards.

One by one, each of the children experimented with the activities John and Betty had forbidden them to try. They found that many of these activities were quite enjoyable and did not bring dire results, other than provoking their parents' anger. Family communication deteriorated. On one issue after another, John and Betty were confronted with questions about the logic of their standards. Both they and their children recognized that the explanations were inadequate.

As the children graduated and moved out of their parents' home, John and Betty lost their last remnant of parental control. Because of the lifestyles their children had adopted, John and Betty concluded that their sons and daughters had turned away from their faith and rejected Christ. Gradually, the children, too, began to describe themselves as non-Christians. John and Betty were left alone with the empty feeling that although they had done what was right, the church and society had not supported them. They felt they were among the last parents to try to uphold Christian standards for their children. And they believed their efforts had been sabotaged by a compromising church and worldly schools.

When we demand obedience, we attempt to use the law to motivate behavior, which leads to legalism. In contrast, teaching submission is part of the gospel: the good news that one can choose his or her own course of action without threatening a valued relationship. Clearly, parents who expect submission rather than demanding unquestioning obedience are not "lording it over" their children but are acting as their servants.

The responsibility for teaching the attitude of submission rests squarely on parents. To be effective teachers, parents must not be mastered by their own anger when their children disobey. Rather, they must learn to discuss differences of perspective with their children without feeling that their authority is necessarily being challenged. They must affirm to their children that their love is not diminished by the disagreement, or even by disobedience. Parents need to express their desire to keep the relationship intact whatever the outcome, and to help their children see that inner motives and attitudes are more important than outward behavior (though outward behavior flows from inner motives—Matt. 6). By respecting the child in a conflict, parents model the respect and submission they expect the child to return to them (Eph. 5:21).

When submission (rather than obedience) characterizes the parent-child relationship, parents are actually less likely to encounter disobedience. Submission encourages a spirit of cooperation. Each request that a parent makes of a child, then, becomes an expectation of working together for everyone's benefit rather than a contest for control. Children who know their opinions and perspectives are respected and welcomed can engage in conversation and persuasion rather than in rebellion, power struggles, and manipulation.

Of course, children, with their fallen, old natures, may be disagreeable and disobedient in rebellion rather than in submission. The parents' role then becomes one of calling for respect but not for conformity. For example, a parent might say, "You are free to express why you disagree with my position or decision, but you must express your disagreement calmly and without attacking me as a person." Similarly, a parent may say, "You may choose not to do what I am requesting, but you will then have to deal with the consequences." These consequences may range from confining young children to their rooms when they run in the street, to shutting off television for those who do not complete their homework, to taking the car keys from teenage drivers who do not return at the agreed-upon time.

Going to the Movies

The Appletons were eating supper on Friday night. Thirteen-year-old Drew injected this announcement into the conversation: "I'm going out with the guys tonight. Tim's dad will drive us to the movie and pick us up."

"Not so fast, young man," jumped in Mr. Appleton. "You may ask for permission, but you can't just presume to tell us what you're doing. You have to learn to check before you make plans. Now tell me what's up."

"Well, Tim, Mark, Steve, and I all want to get out after this week of school. We had lots of tests, and we need a break."

"But you didn't know if we had plans for the family. How about a break with your family?"

"Dad, that's no break! You know, not like being with my friends. Besides you don't have any plans, do you?"

"Well, I guess not, but we could play a game."

Debbie, Drew's fifteen-year-old sister, jumped in now. "Oh, Dad, that's so boring. Just let him go."

Mrs. Appleton threw in her thoughts too. "Bill, it's not worth a fight. If he wants to go out, and you make him stay in, we won't have any fun anyway."

"I guess I'm outnumbered. Well, what movie are you going to see?"

Drew shrugged, "We haven't decided yet. We're going down to the Super Eight, so we can choose what seems good when we get there. If we make it by seven o'clock, we can choose any of them. We've got to find one none of us have seen before."

"I don't think I like that idea," frowned Mr. Appleton. "I think you need a definite plan. That's how trouble gets started— when you don't know what you're doing. Debbie, would you get the entertainment section of last night's newspaper? I want to see what's playing. . . . Hmmm. A couple of R-rated movies. You know you can't try to sneak into those. Uhh. . . . Several of these are rated PG-13. I don't think you should consider those either."

"Dad, I am thirteen. I can handle it."

"You know what they say about computers. GIGO—garbage in, garbage out. You don't need to put garbage into your mind on purpose."

Debbie spoke up again, "Just because a movie is rated PG-13 or even R doesn't mean that it's garbage."

"Just listen to this. `Adult themes and violent scenes.' Even adults don't need that for entertainment."

"Aw, Dad, it's just reality," whined Drew.

"You get enough of that on the news. I think you need to stick to G or PG movies."

"That's embarrassing. The guys will think I'm a baby."

"Bill, see if there's anything there that is okay." Mrs. Appleton was trying to find a way out of the conflict.

"This one only says, `profanity.' Why do you need to hear a bunch of cussing, especially if they're taking the Lord's name in vain?" Dad was looking for some support now.

Debbie's matter-of-fact voice came on again. "He's heard all those words before. It's not like he'll start talking that way just because he hears it again in a movie."

"Maybe not, but I still think we Christians need to exercise some judgment about what we accept for ourselves."

Mrs. Appleton suggested another strategy. "Drew, what if we trust you to make a good decision with your friends tonight, on the condition that you *agree to a conference with us tomorrow. At that conference, we'll try to work out a list of standards for entertainment for our family. It will take work, but I think we're smart enough to come up with something we can all be satisfied with."*

This conversation has the ingredients to move toward a demand for unquestioning obedience. Mr. Appleton has the power to enforce his wishes and shut down the discussion. In addition to his power as a parent, he can use spiritual arguments. Faced with similar situations some Christians have felt that blanket rules, such as "we just don't go to movies," simplify the issue and avoid the risks of these sorts of exchanges.

On the other hand, this conversation could also fuel the engine of respectful submission. Mr. Appleton could model willingness to listen and learn without jumping to conclusions, opening the way for Drew to learn from his father. Drew has the opportunity to learn the criteria and processes underlying responsible, Christian decision-making. He also has the chance to practice disagreeing respectfully. The input of Debbie and Mrs. Appleton can either confuse the issue and damage relationships or reinforce the family's ability to work together to solve problems.

Mr. Appleton and Drew are headed for a clash that could strain other family relationships as well. Mr. Appleton may try to head off further trouble in one of two ways: by demanding unquestioning obedience or by fostering healthy submission. How might he respond to Mrs. Appleton's suggestion, taking each approach?

To demand obedience, Mr. Appleton can say, "

"

A predictable response from Drew would be, "

"

To foster submission, Mr. Appleton can say, "

"

A predictable response from Drew would be, "

"

On what issues can Mr. Appleton and Drew profitably discuss their differences of opinion?

What might be the consequences if Mr. Appleton and Drew do not work out these differences?

In what ways can Mr. Appleton influence Drew while building his son's sense of personal responsibility?

What attitudes and values can Mr. Appleton cultivate in Drew and in himself by intentionally making use of servant authority in this conversation?

Discipline or Punishment?

What is the place of discipline and punishment? How do parents guide their children to self-disciplined maturity?

When parents discipline their children, they should do so with the goal of helping their children grow rather than making them "pay" for something they did wrong. The character of a given parent-child relationship is not determined by the conflicts between them, but by the way in which they resolve those conflicts. Discipline that seeks growth rather than punishment rests only on a biblical sense of forgiveness. Punishment tends to divide and separate (in fact, the ultimate punishment is separation from God), while discipline unites, expresses love, and stimulates growth (Prov. 3:12; Heb. 12:6-10; Rev. 3:19).

The issue of physical (corporal) "punishment," primarily spanking, is a significant question for Christians in the exercise of parental authority. On the popular level, it has been the battleground between authoritarian and permissive parents for years. Authoritarian parents insist that the child receives some intrinsic value by having pain administered at frequent intervals. Permissive parents, on the other hand, feel that any such "punishment" is harmful to the child and counterproductive to positive teaching about handling personal difficulty. Awareness of child abuse has generated both legitimate concern and considerable anxiety and fear for parents. Scripture speaks to this matter in a way that reflects neither of these popular views of authority.

In Old Testament times parents were clearly expected to use a rod to correct and train their children (Prov. 13:24; 23:13; 29:15; etc.). To escape this conclusion would require extreme exegetical contortions. Admittedly the words sound harsh to twentieth-century ears: rod, hate, beat. However, they are also coupled with the ideas of love, patience, training, and correction.

When seen as part of parents' servant authority, physical punishment may play a meaningful role in moving children toward maturity—as long as it adheres to the biblical model:

First, physical punishment should not be used to make children "pay" for wrong. The New Testament clearly teaches that no human being can pay a sufficient penalty for his or her sin. That is exactly the point of Christ's substitutionary atonement. Rather such punishment should be directed at the growth and learning of the child.

Second, physical punishment should not be an expression of the parents' whims or personal desires but rather an expression of the parents' service to the child.

Third, the pain of physical punishment has no intrinsic value of its own; its value is evident only when directed toward specific growth.

Fourth, physical punishment is not an appropriate outlet for uncontrolled anger or parental frustration.

Fifth, physical discipline may be chosen when other consequences are inappropriate.

The Snowball Incident

Mr. Kelley came home from work early because of the snowstorm. He brewed a cup of tea and sat down to read the newspaper. Just then the doorbell rang. A policeman stood there with eight-year-old Joe.

"Is this your son, sir?" asked the officer. "He was hiding behind the hedge at the park, throwing snowballs at passing cars. Some bigger kids were with him, but I couldn't catch up to them. Since no one was hurt and no one complained, I'll just leave him with you if you'll promise to give him what he deserves."

If Mr. Kelley thinks in terms of punishment, what could he conclude that Joe deserves?

If Mr. Kelley thinks in terms of discipline, how might his strategy change?

Think of a list of possible consequences that Joe could face. Classify each of them as discipline or punishment.

Discipline   Punishment

What qualities of responsibility and maturity do you think Mr. Kelley should seek to cultivate in the way he disciplines Joe?

How do you think Mr. Kelley felt when he saw Joe at the door with the police officer? How could he express his feelings appropriately and constructively to Joe?

Conflict Resolution

Because both parents and children are imperfect, many parent-child conflicts can best be addressed in terms similar to those in 1 Corinthians 6 for conflicts between believers. In these situations both parties confront each other directly. Each one expresses his or her viewpoint on the situation. Every effort is made to resolve the differences as rapidly as possible with equity and due process for all concerned. In the church, the unity of the Body of Christ is at stake. Between parents and children, the unity of the family is at stake. In each case, diligent effort to negotiate is required on both sides.

In the family the greater burden of understanding, maturity, and effort rests on parents. Parents are responsible to exercise authority for conflict resolution, but they must do so in a manner that reflects their servant authority. That's where *no-lose* conflict resolution comes into play. By following the orderly steps of this approach to solving conflicts, parents and children negotiate their differences until they arrive at a solution that satisfies both parties. To use the approach effectively, parents must use listening skills to ascertain accurately their child's perspective and help the child evaluate his or her own position. They must send accurate "I" messages so that the child understands the parents' expectations and feelings.

Though several variations to this approach are possible, steps used by business management for problem solving and decision making form a basic pattern or plan to follow. Here is the version of these steps presented by Thomas Gordon in *Parent Effectiveness Training*[1]:

1. Identify and define the conflict.
2. Generate possible alternative solutions.
3. Evaluate the alternative solutions.
4. Decide on the best acceptable solution.
5. Work out ways of implementing the solution.
6. Follow up to evaluate how it worked.

The way parents handle conflicts says a lot about their stance toward the authority they exercise on God's behalf.

Authoritarian parents engage in power struggles with their children. They seek to win compliance with their wishes by exerting pressure or force (physical, mental, or social). If they do not win, they feel their authority is threatened. Permissive parents, on the other hand, seek to avoid using power by avoiding conflicts. The result may be that their children will use power and force to pressure parents to get their way, and the permissive parents will give in to avoid conflict.

However, conflict is not necessarily bad; it can be the arena in which great parent-child relationships and personal responsibility are developed. Parents exercising servant authority do not avoid conflicts simply for comfort's sake. Whenever possible, they negotiate conflicts so that both parent and child are satisfied with the resolution of the problem. Often mutual understanding is enough to resolve the difficulty.

As the authority, the parent sets the pace by expressing respect for the child's personhood, needs, and viewpoint. Parents also expect children to respect their personhood and authority as received from God. Although the parents are one party when negotiations are needed, they are also in charge of the negotiation. By virtue of delegated authority, parents are responsible to conduct the negotiations for conflict resolution and to do it with justice.

Get together with one or more of your children. Together think of a recent conflict you now feel comfortable talking about. Use the following steps to practice negotiating a resolution to that conflict.

First, describe the conflict here.

Now work through the conflict again using the steps.

1. Identify and define the conflict.

2. Generate possible alternative solutions.

3. Evaluate the alternative solutions.

4. Decide on the best acceptable solution.

5. Work out ways of implementing the solution.

6. Follow up to evaluate how it worked.

When Nothing Works

Despite all of a parent's good intentions and efforts at resolving conflicts so no one loses, in some situations servant authority demands strong action that may not be agreed to or appreciated by the child at the time.

Urgency

While most of the pain children experience as they learn to make their own decisions turns out to be profitable, occasionally the consequences are just too severe for a parent to tolerate. In very young children, playing with knives, matches, and electrical sockets or running in the street are such examples. The risk of injuries and possible death are too high for a parent or child to pay while learning. As the one charged with the responsibility to exercise authority, the parent acts decisively and immediately. For the safety of the child, physical restraint may be necessary.

When the Parent Is Held Responsible

In a few areas God and society hold parents responsible for the actions of their children. Socially, property and personal damage usually fall into this category. Parents can be held legally and financially responsible for their children's actions. In these cases parents have both the responsibility and obligation to insist on their children's cooperation. Though Christian parents exercise authority in a very different way than secular authorities, they are responsible to teach their children to be submissive and respectful to secular authorities: police, teachers, and the like. The attitude of submission and respect must persist even in those situations where the secular authority is unjust and where conscious disobedience is required.

In the moral, ethical arena the problem is not quite as simple. Parents cannot determine their children's morality, but they can strongly influence it. However, in some cases they have a clear moral responsibility in the matter. The example of Eli's sons in 1 Samuel 2:12ff illustrates this principle. Eli was responsible for the operation of the tabernacle. God condemned him because he did not restrain his sons from their immoral and unjust living, particularly in connection with their conduct of worship. If the sons chose to continue to be rebellious in spirit, Eli could do nothing about that. However, he was responsible for their priestly roles and could have forbidden them to conduct worship.

Another example is more contemporary but no less extreme. A young person is sexually promiscuous. If the teen is bent on continuing that behavior into adulthood, parents cannot stop him or her. However, they need not allow the young person to hold group orgies in their home. A confrontation ("I" message) in these situations, where the parents explain clearly just how strongly they feel about a given issue and why, may be God's way of calling the child to repent. Parents cannot maintain their integrity and ignore immoral and unethical behavior by their children.

Stalemates

Despite all the good-faith bargaining that may be done in negotiating conflicts between parents and children, not all conflicts will be solved. In these instances parents must exercise their servant authority carefully but clearly. Stalemates can result from several things. Perhaps the children do not want to solve the conflict; they are rebellious and resist parental efforts to negotiate. Perhaps the parents' demands are unrealistic. Perhaps one or both are too lazy to do the hard work of negotiation. Sometimes either the parent or the child may wish to have power over the other and be unwilling to cooperate. All of these are the result of sin in either the parent or the child or both. Whether laziness or rebellion or power-greed, the problem is still sin.

Because sin is the source of these stalemates, the parent must be careful but clear in exercising authority in these situations. Careful because the parent's sin may be the problem. Clear because when children sin, they need to be confronted.

Go for the Best

In our concern to be responsible parents, we may be tempted to be strict out of fear of not providing a high-enough standard with a supportive-enough structure. We can be trapped by this paradox because we don't want our children to flounder with the insufficient direction that comes from being too relaxed or too permissive. Thus judgment, unquestioning obedience, and punishment are attractive. Unfortunately, these are counterfeits of the much more substantial, challenging, and enduring patterns of confrontation, submission, and discipline. As Christian parents, we can't afford to accept inadequate allurement; we must insist on the authentic currency of parental authority.

Suggestions for Group Session

Opening

All parents are interested in swapping discipline techniques. Start out your time together by having some fun with this. Each person can suggest their favorite, "most creative and effective" discipline techniques. These can be techniques their parents used on them or that they have used with their own children. Make this a lighthearted time. A humorous way to conclude this activity is to choose the group's favorite technique by informally gauging the enthusiasm of applause for each choice.

One person can open your formal group time by praying for the ability to distinguish biblical concepts from other ideas. A more personal prayer time will come at the close of this session.

For Discussion

1. Divide into four groups. Assign each group one of the New Testament passages that deals with church discipline. As these subgroups examine their assigned passages, they should look for principles that could be applied to parents' relationships with their children. Each group should record its findings and be ready to report. Consider the topics of this chapter to help identify principles to share: confrontation, submission, discipline, and conflict resolution.

   Group 1   Matthew 18:15-20
   Group 2   1 Corinthians 5
   Group 3   1 Corinthians 6:1-11
   Group 4   2 Corinthians 1:23-2:11

   Each group should post their sheet where everyone can see it when they report their findings.

2. Together compare and contrast church discipline with family discipline, keeping in mind the principles just presented. In what ways are church discipline and parents' discipline of children similar, and in what ways are they different? Writing two lists in parallel columns on a chalkboard is a good way to keep track of the input.

3. Have a couple of volunteers role-play the conversation between Julie and her mother from the exercise on pages 64-65. An entertaining and challenging way to do this is by having two people start the conversation using a judgmental approach. After a couple of minutes, another volunteer can take the mother's role and try to switch the approach to confrontation. After another couple of minutes, a fourth volunteer can take Julie's role.

    Debrief the role-play by first asking each participant to describe his or her emotional responses as the conversation developed. Then the group can offer their observations of what transpired and make suggestions for more effective confrontation.

4. Take a couple of minutes to review responses to the exercise following the Appleton's struggle over "Going to the Movies" (pp. 69-70). Form clusters of three to five people. Each subgroup selects one incident from their own families that involves a decision between submission and demanded obedience. They then come up with one piece of advice they would give to other parents who want to cultivate healthy, biblical submission in their children. These may be compiled and duplicated.

5. Think of an incident in which you had to decide between punishing and disciplining one of your children. Compare this experience with your response to the "Snowball Incident" (p. 71). Discuss with your group the qualities of maturity and responsibility you are working to develop in your children through your discipline strategies.

6. Two volunteers agree to work through a parent-child conflict with the group coaching them through the steps of no-lose conflict resolution. A good way to select the situation is to ask the first volunteer to take the child's role and describe a conflict situation. Then another person can volunteer to take the role of the parent. As they work through the steps, the group as a whole can add their ideas, suggestions, and input. Keep the conversation moving quickly so that you get a feel for the flow of the process, rather than getting bogged down in the details of any one step.

7. Read about and discuss the difficulties Eli and Samuel had with their adult children in 1 Samuel 2:12-25 and 8:1-5.

Closing

Samuel's painful experience with his children confronts us with the risks and challenges of properly using our parental authority with our children, especially as they become adults and are more independent. With this backdrop, get together in little groups to pray for your children.

[1] Gordon, Thomas. *Parent Effectiveness Training*. New York: New American Library, 1970, p. 237ff.

FIVE

BEING IN CHARGE WHEN YOU CAN'T BE IN CONTROL

Follow the history of Fred and Jean Thomas' oldest son, James. He was born into a conservative, close-knit Christian family. His father was a laborer who worked hard for a modest income that allowed few luxuries. Although neither of his parents had any education beyond high school, education was highly valued in the home. Fred and Jean were also faithful in church attendance, not just on Sunday morning but at the other gatherings and special events too. From the time they were first married, both Fred and Jean held responsibilities in the church's organization—sometimes teaching Sunday school and other times working with committees.

Like most couples, Fred and Jean were elated when James was born, but they did not have a specific plan for how to raise him. So they relied on patterns from their own homes, which were strongly reinforced by the expectations of their church. Family devotions were a regular bedtime ritual, but skipping on occasion was not considered catastrophic. The Saturday night ritual consisted of baths and Sunday school lessons. When Jean felt James was ready, or if she felt the subjects were important, she would lecture her son about Christian values and behavior. Sometimes her comments were an explanation of the importance of only marrying a Christian or finding a career that God would approve of. At other times they were an explanation of the behavior standards that Christians in their particular church considered important.

James tolerated these lectures, but felt they were stiff and artificial. He often felt like saying, "I know that already!" But somehow the lectures never prevented him from opening up to his mother. Particularly as he reached his teen years, he would tell his mother what he was doing in school and how he was feeling. She would listen patiently while fixing supper or washing dishes, never saying much. Though it didn't happen as often, James liked to talk to his father too.

James did well enough in high school to go away to college. The family scraped together enough money to get him started. He worked part-time to pay the rest. In college James met up with people and ideas he had never even heard of in his small, conservative church back home. He struggled with deciding if he wanted to be a Christian like his parents. He struggled with knowing whether the faith he had was really his own, or if it was just something he had accepted from his parents. When he came home from school, James shared some of his new thoughts with his parents, but kept some of the most important ones to himself. He didn't want to scare his parents. He wasn't sure he could defend himself against the Bible verses his mother would quote. But his mom and dad listened and didn't say much to him.

Now James is married and raising his own children. Listen to what he says about what influence his parents had on him, and how he thinks it will affect the way he raises his own children:

We always knew we were Christians, and that was somehow special. I loved my parents and didn't want to hurt them in any way. My mother's lectures annoyed me, and I didn't pay too much attention to our family devotions. I guess I did learn something from those enforced Saturday night Sunday school lessons, though. I was about the only one in the class who ever did them. I really enjoyed some of the Sunday school teachers, but Sunday school itself was dull.

I probably learned the most about what being a Christian was by the casual comments my parents made. When my parents observed something particularly commendable or reprehensible, they would make an observation about it, usually to each other. And they appeared to me to live by all the principles they expressed about others. I thought they were perfect saints.

I can't remember them making negative comments about me, even when I disobeyed seriously. I enjoyed talking to them. I felt sure I would not be scolded for saying something I really felt, but sometimes I would keep it in for fear of what they might think. This was especially true when I came home from college. Nevertheless, their willingness to listen to me really helped me figure out what I was experiencing and believing.

In college I realized just how important church was to them and me. I continued the habit of my childhood, almost without thinking. I went to church regularly and even taught Sunday school, but all the while I was struggling with my own faith. From my college experience I learned that the church is Christian fellowship, not just dull meetings. I'm not as conservative as they were, and I have modified a few of the values that were important to them. But I think I'm basically working on the same thing they were: following Jesus.

If I could do half as well with my children as they did with me, I'd be happy. Their willingness to listen to me was very important. And it wasn't just that they listened, but they really seemed to accept that I had my own ideas and could think for myself.

Of course, they let me know what they wanted for me too. I clearly understood what they thought was good for a Christian and what wasn't. Sometimes I think that our family devotions could have been more helpful to me, but I don't know that the child-oriented things that we do now around our table are much more productive.

I think I felt that I could accept their values more easily because they were willing to let me have my own values and were available to talk about them. I hope I can be as clear about what I believe with my children and still give them the opportunity to form their own beliefs. Of course, I want them to follow Jesus too. I will be hurt if they reject Christ, and I will grieve. But I know I can't accept him for them.

Think back over your own childhood. Try to write a similar but shorter history of your upbringing. What did your parents do to instill their values in you? What are you doing the same or differently to communicate your values to your own children?

Authority and Values

Conflicts between parents and children over needs and desires are tough enough to deal with, but conflicts over values can be monumental. By definition, values are something we hold dear, and parents earnestly seek and desire that their children hold values similar to their own. Christian parents particularly have a sense of the importance of some absolute values based on the teachings of Scripture. For these values to be rejected by children is a sizable tragedy. Yet attempts to coerce values into children by using power not only fail, but frequently bring about rebellion.

Does this mean that Christian parents cannot teach their values to their children? Of course not! Such teaching is a responsibility specifically committed to parents in Scripture (Deut. 6; Prov. 22:6; Eph. 6). Deuteronomy 6:7 expresses the key principle for this kind of teaching: "Impress them [God's laws] on your children. Talk about them when you sit at home and when you walk along the road, when you lie down and when you get up."

In other words, make conversation about spiritual values a routine part of everyday living. Look for the "teachable moments" in daily events. Create teaching opportunities from the special occasions that life offers.

For example, if we take advantage of it, television can be a wonderful catalyst for Christian parents to use to teach values. My older boys and I have had some marvelous conversations prompted by beer commercials during sports programs. Why is it that women are absent when "it doesn't get any better than this?" And if they are there, they are cartoon playthings for the men, not real people for personal relationships. Old Milwaukee has helped me talk with my boys about a biblical view of the dignity and personhood of women, how to treat women with courtesy and respect, the place of alcohol in the life of a disciple of Jesus, and the things that really make life satisfying.

In most of our lives, the opportunities for "values conversations" are limitless. Supper talk about current events is the vehicle for conveying values about peace and war, poverty and wealth, law and authority, integrity and trust, nationalism and the global community of the church. Events in our lives—from the death of a pet to an unwed pregnancy, from the purchase of a car to spring garden clean-up—are value-laden opportunities, if we as parents will intentionally take advantage of them. No artificial application of an abstract or moralistic Bible lesson is required. Life and truth are inseparably integrated.

Actually, we cannot avoid teaching values to our children in these settings. If we are silent, our children still gather lessons such as, "This is too sensitive to talk about," or, "Mom and Dad don't care about this," or, "I'm going to have to figure out what's right and wrong on my own."

Use the categories of Deuteronomy 6:7 to think of some opportunities for talking about values in your family. Write your ideas here.

1. When You Sit at Home—Opportunities for discussing values at home:

Opportunity	Value to Discuss
a.	
b.	
c.	
d.	
e.	

2. When You Walk Along the Road—Opportunities for discussing values when you are away from home:

Opportunity	Value to Discuss
a.	
b.	
c.	
d.	
e.	

3. When You Lie Down—Opportunities for discussing values in your evening routines:

Opportunity   Value to Discuss

a.

b.

c.

d.

e.

4. When You Get Up—Opportunities for discussing values in your morning routines:

Opportunity   Value to Discuss

a.

b.

c.

d.

e.

Grace and Law Again

Combined with some informal "research" of his own, Philip Yancey analyzes the work done by Merton Strommen's Youth Research Center in an article in *Moody Monthly* magazine. This research points out why attempts to coerce values often lead to tragedy and suggests how this is related to the parents' law or gospel orientation. Researchers asked parents and their teenage children to answer a series of identical questions, then also asked parents to predict how their teenagers would answer. "Low correlating parents [less accurate predictors of their children's answers] tended to view Christianity as a religion of works—something one did. The high correlating parents [more accurate predictors of their children's answers] tended to view Christianity as religion of grace—something one accepts as a gift."[1] In short, children of gospel-oriented parents tended to adopt more of their parents' values than children of legalistic parents.

We've already looked at how law and gospel work when behavior is the issue. The law calls for confrontation ("I" message) when standards or rights have been violated. The gospel calls for empathic listening for guilt or other distress when someone asks for forgiveness. When values are involved, the strategy is more complex and the risks are higher. Grace-oriented parents recognize a fundamental equality of fallenness with their children. They know that while they may be more mature than their children, their status before God also is utterly dependent on receiving mercy from Jesus Christ. Thus, they have no pretensions of moral superiority over their children. As those who are recipients of God's forgiveness, they are eager to extend forgiveness to their children. Thus, children need not fear that even behavior with severe consequences will deprive them of loving relationships with their parents.

Perhaps the greatest test of parents' commitment to grace comes when parents have wronged their children and seek their forgiveness. This is when children learn the profound reality of the gospel. This is where parents gain the credibility that makes a grace orientation so powerful in values formation. Through this process, children learn that right and wrong have an objective reality independent of their parents' feelings and opinions.

When children are confident in the loving relationships they have with their parents, they gain a freedom to explore with their parents the moral and value issues that are real to them. If children can expect anger or shock when they ask if sex outside of marriage is really wrong or question if God is real, they will invariably keep those questions to themselves. On the other hand, children who have asked for and been given forgiveness in behavioral areas will feel a freedom to raise more troublesome value issues. In fact, grace itself is foundational for coping with the harsh realities of life. Only through grace can we face disappointment in others and failure in ourselves, and still be able to continue with a constructive and positive outlook.

Brian's parents had devoted themselves to demanding ministry careers. When he finished high school, he moved a considerable distance from them. Though he did not reject their faith, he drifted far from viewing Christ as the central focus of his life and avoided Christian fellowship. During that time he met Susan, who was trying to get away from her secular and dysfunctional family. Their relationship became a fellowship of escape that drew them into increasing intimacy. As might be expected, Susan was soon pregnant. Brian and Susan married quickly without their families and with very few friends.

With considerable apprehension, Brian called his parents to set up a visit to introduce Susan to them. Through their tears came not a hint of condemnation. Instead they congratulated their son and assured him of their support. Before the visit, Brian's mother wrote a letter to Susan, welcoming her into the family. She told her new daughter-in-law she could hardly wait to get to know her and to have a new grandchild. Susan has treasured that letter ever since.

During that visit, Brian asked his parents to forgive him for letting them down and not living up to what they had taught him. In the ensuing conversation, Susan asked how she could resolve her guilt feelings, especially since she had never experienced forgiveness in her own family. Brian's parents explained how to trust Jesus for forgiveness. That was the beginning of a new life of faith for Susan and discipleship for Brian. Before they died, Brian's parents saw Brian and Susan become leaders in their church, and saw their grandchildren grow in Christian faith.

Don't get the wrong idea. Grace does not mean overlooking wrong behavior or values. (If Brian had persisted in immoral living and refused to ask for forgiveness, his parents would have needed to confront and admonish him.) Rather, grace is the means by which God keeps us in relationship with himself and each other, even though we fail at and even reject the good God wants for us. Grace is only effective when wrong is acknowledged. However, as Brian's parents sensed, once wrong is confessed, not to extend grace is to wallow in the past and stay stuck in sin.

Christian admonition is made in a spirit of humble service, seeking restoration and growth. It is done in a spirit of gentleness and with a desire to help the other involved (Gal. 6:1-2). It is also done with a willingness to be admonished in return for mutual benefit. Children will be willing to receive admonition if the relationship is open, right, and if the parents themselves are living the values they are attempting to teach.

A grace orientation values the relationship above what the child does. In it parents live out God's initiative in pursuing those who are in revolt against him. Jesus declared that he came to seek and save the lost (Luke 19:10), as a physician for the spiritually sick (Luke 5:31). Paul asserts that while we were his powerless, sinful enemies, Christ died for us (Rom. 5:6-10). Thus, when children choose values that stand at odds with their parents' values, the parents can use their servant authority to continue to pursue a healthy relationship with their children. This does not imply approving unrighteous lifestyles, but is rather a step of faith that never gives up on God's ability to bring change.

While the foundations of values are laid in early childhood, the crises of values tend to emerge in late adolescence and early adulthood. That was certainly true for Bill and Martha.

On graduating from high school, their son Doug joined the military to get away from the religious values of his parents. He found a group of friends with whom he could seek thrills in drinking, drugs, and promiscuous sex. Once out of the military, Doug lost even more control and was arrested for drug possession. Bill bailed him out of jail and kept in touch through the trial process.

With that behind him, Doug moved in with Nancy. Bill and Martha included Doug and Nancy in family gatherings, and tried to encourage them to get married without nagging. More than five years later, Doug and Nancy were married and began attending worship. A couple of years later, Nancy told the family she had come to trust Christ and wanted to join the church. After hearing Nancy talk enthusiastically about her new faith, Doug sought pastoral help in renewing his Christian commitment. Some time later, they joined the high school ministry team as assistant youth leaders.

Through years of disappointment and pain, Bill and Martha persisted in keeping the relationship open with Doug without compromising their values. This kind of persistence requires a faith perspective, because such ef-

forts are not always rewarded with success. Bill and Martha are still work-
ing to cultivate a redemptive relationship with another son who is distant
from them and from the Lord.

Think about the sorts of values you want your children to adopt. Look at the list of typical values for Christian parents below. Rank them from most important (1) to least important (10).

_____ attend church regularly
_____ date or marry a committed Christian
_____ succeed in school or career
_____ save sex for marriage
_____ live out faith in Christ
_____ pursue a ministry career (pastorate, missions, etc.)
_____ abstain from destructive habits (gambling, drugs, tobacco, etc.)
_____ become a leader in church or community (school, profession, politics)
_____ be a courteous person with good manners
_____ have a positive, thankful outlook on life

Now develop your own list of ten values you want your children to adopt and rank them from 1 to 10. You may repeat things from the previous list, if you wish.

_____
_____
_____
_____
_____
_____
_____
_____
_____
_____

Examine your value rankings in light of law and gospel. In what ways do you think a grace orientation is most evident in your parenting?

In what ways do you think you could strengthen the grace orientation in your parenting?

More than a Good Example

Even all of this is not enough. While teaching and modeling can lay the foundation, the most important times of value development come during what Jean Piaget called "disequilibration." Ted Ward explains this process for Christian parents[2]:

Especially in the moral and ethical realm, a learner encounters many experiences that he or she cannot handle from the point of view of pattern [previously experienced] dilemmas [that] can lead to a dawning of awareness that "there's more to it than that." Sometimes they lead to doubts. The old formula for judging right and wrong doesn't seem to cover this case very well, and even if it does, it isn't as clear-cut as it once seemed.

Upon realizing that a member of the family is encountering such a period of disequilibration, the model-oriented or rule-wielding parent will likely tend to swing into action to quickly restabilize the "drifting" person. Perhaps just as bad is the "teacher" orientation that causes some to rush in and attempt to prematurely reequilibrate the person at a new and higher stage of development.

Instead parents are teachers who should join the learner to explore the disequilibration with him, to look for other instances of the dilemma, to consider why the previous value structure is becoming inadequate, and in general, to provide a comfortable and honest sounding board for the person in disequilibration. From a growing sense of disequilibration, ultimately the awareness of the next higher structure emerges to fill the gap. Christians know the process; it isn't magic or sourceless; it is a built-in human attribute. The apostle Paul writes about it [though in reference to a criticism of the wicked] in Romans 1:19-20.

So when it comes to value development, parents cannot appeal to force and expect their children to come out with the same beliefs they hold. Rather the parents' authority can be used to establish an atmosphere and relationship with their children that will allow them to take important steps toward value development. No matter what the parents do, however, they cannot guarantee the results in advance. Parenting implies risk. By using force and power, parents can coerce their children into external conformity (which often turns out to be counterproductive to the values they are attempting to develop), but ultimately children must choose their own values. Parents who use biblical servant authority can reduce the risks and assist their children in making these choices wisely, but parents cannot make a meaningful choice of values for their children.

The summers before our older sons entered junior high school, I took each of them camping for a special one-on-one father-son campout in the New Jersey Pine Barrens. I wanted a chance to talk to each of them about the changes they would be going through in the coming years. I wanted them to realize that coming up with answers would not always be easy.

As we talked, I went through some of the areas where these problems were likely to arise: friends, personal changes in puberty, school and career decision-making, sex and dating and marriage, understanding what is happening in the world, seeing problems in the church, the development of mature faith, and knowing right from wrong. I admitted that I didn't have solutions for all of these problems, but I would be happy to listen and talk about their questions.

Those were great campouts, filled with conversation. I didn't have to set any further agenda because my sons asked questions about the issues that concerned me. Instead of giving answers, I added my questions to theirs. In a sense, these events marked the start of adult-to-adult relationships with my sons.

Expectations

Often parents are aware of exercising their authority only in a conflict or when they anticipate a conflict. While the way authority is being exercised becomes most clear in a conflict, parents who have healthy, positive relationships with their children will exercise their authority in the same way most of the time.

Parents have goals for their children. Some of these are negative: things the parents want their children to avoid. Others are positive: things parents want their children to experience. The most important of these goals for Christian parents are those related to the development of biblical values in their children.

When children achieve the goals their parents have for them, parents are exercising their authority in what may be its most potent form. Some children *do* respond positively to parental authority. The likelihood of a positive response increases when the parent's attitude is that of the servant and the relationship with the child is constructive.

Another important quality of parental authority is expectation—that is, *expecting* your children to do what you have in mind. This confidence is expressed in an attitude of "taking charge," recognizing that the authority delegated by God to parents is a real and serious responsibility. The servant authority attitude expects that instructions will be followed, but it is quite different from the "lording it over" spirit that characterizes authoritarian parenting. And the expectation that commands be fulfilled makes it different from permissive parenting.

List here ways in which your children are fulfilling the expectations you have for them.

Name of Child:
Expectations:

Name of Child:
Expectations:

Name of Child:
Expectations:

Name of Child:
Expectations:

Name of Child:
Expectations:

Name of Child:
Expectations:

Assessing Maturity

Another way of looking at the issue of values is as the development of mature character—the goal of nurture in the life of the church. The purpose of the spiritual gifts Paul discusses in Ephesians 4 is that "we all reach unity in the faith and in the knowledge of the Son of God and become mature, attaining to the whole measure of the fullness of Christ" (v. 13). Paul identifies the purpose of his teaching ministry as presenting everyone as mature in Christ (Col. 1:28). If Christian parents see that they are also God's means of cultivating maturity, then they can take their cue from this parallel with the church's task.

The character of Christ is our model and measure of maturity. Scripture offers several portraits and principles for both the church and parents to guide the development of Christlike maturity. In Mark 10:45, Jesus describes the purpose of his ministry—serving and giving himself as a ransom. This suggests that the core of mature, Christlike character is serving others. Thus, parental authority that is characterized by humble service is consistent with what it seeks to develop in children. Parents live what they seek if they use their authority in a biblically consistent fashion.

Humble service is the single most characteristic quality of Christlike maturity. It is the overarching principle that organizes the specific traits that God is seeking in people. Similarly, it is the guiding focus for parents. Scripture provides a detailed portrait of the humble servant:

- The inventory of the fruit of the Spirit in Galatians 5:22-23 forms a kind of evaluation checklist for servanthood.

- Romans 12:9-21 is a sort of nuts-and-bolts instruction sheet for the mature servant.

- The Sermon on the Mount (Matt. 5-7) is a comprehensive discussion of the lifestyle of the mature servant disciple.

Studying these Scriptures raises an intriguing line of thinking. Maturity is a developmental process. It is not an objective achievement that can be attained once and for all, like memorizing the multiplication tables. In fact, it changes over time. What would be mature behavior for a one-year-old (e.g., eating with the fingers) would be immature for a six-year-old. Similarly, willingness to share a toy might indicate maturity for a six-year-old, but would be an inadequate measure for a sixteen-year-old. A way to think about this is to ask, "What does it mean to be appropriately mature at a given age, whether two or ten or thirty?" Or, even more probing: "What does it mean to be Christlike at a given age: eight, twelve, or fifty?"

Maturity is difficult to measure. Examine one or more of the Scripture passages on maturity listed above. Then, in the spaces provided below, list five behaviors you believe indicate maturity and five behaviors you believe indicate immaturity.

Behaviors that indicate maturity:

_____ 1.
_____ 2.
_____ 3.
_____ 4.
_____ 5.

Behaviors that indicate immaturity:

_____ 1.
_____ 2.
_____ 3.
_____ 4.
_____ 5.

Now score yourself on these behaviors in the spaces to the left of the numbers. Use 5 as the highest possible score and 1 as the lowest, taking into account the frequency and ease with which you do each listed behavior. Now total the scores in each column and subtract the immaturity score from the maturity score.

This unscientific self-evaluation is designed to help you view yourself, using the same sort of criterion you may be using to assess the maturity of others, particularly your children. If you have been honest with yourself, you will be better able to proceed by looking at your children's maturity more benevolently.

For each of your children, list two of their regular behaviors that you believe indicate their most positive maturity. Then list two of their regular behaviors that you believe show their moments of immaturity.

1. Name of child:
Mature behaviors:
a.
b.
Immature behaviors:
a.
b.

2. Name of child:
Mature behaviors:
a.
b.
Immature behaviors:
a.
b.

3. Name of child:
Mature behaviors:
a.
b.
Immature behaviors:
a.
b.

4. Name of child:
Mature behaviors:
a.
b.
Immature behaviors:
a.
b.

5. Name of child:
Mature behaviors:
a.
b.
Immature behaviors:
a.
b.

6. Name of child:
Mature behaviors:
a.
b.
Immature behaviors:
a.
b.

Now describe in a phrase or brief sentence one thing you have done as a parent to encourage each child's growth toward maturity.

Suggestions for Group Session

Opening

As your group gathers, review the personal history you wrote on how your values were formed in your family (see description on p. 79). Select one thing that you think other people do not know about you or that you think is unique about your experience. Informally circulate in the group, telling several people about how your parents shaped your present values. Also listen to the stories of others. Pay special attention to common themes and distinctive experiences.

At starting time, the whole group should be seated in a circle. Form pairs that do not include spouses (that may require that some couples trade chairs). The people in each pair should pray for each other. Try to tune in to each other's emotional needs in relationships with either parents, children, or both.

For Discussion

1. Go around the circle and have each person identify the one issue in passing values to children that is of greatest concern to him or her. Designate someone to list these issues on newsprint or on a chalkboard. They may be either current questions or those that you anticipate in the future.

2. Read Deuteronomy 6:7. Divide into four groups. Each group should brainstorm opportunities for value discussions and list them on newsprint with a marker. People may start with the lists they prepared on pages 80-81. Group 1 concentrates on opportunities at home, group 2 on those away from home, group 3 on evening routines, and group 4 on morning routines. After developing the list, each group may select its three best ideas to report to the other groups. People may add ideas they can use to their lists on pages 80-81.

3. Stay in the same four groups. Each group works together to identify the five most important values they want to pass on to their children. They may refer to the lists they have ranked on page 84. As each group reports, someone will write the list on the chalkboard. Work as a whole group to select the three highest priority values. Try to do this as a consensus process in which everyone feels satisfied with the results (that can mean revising the original statements).

4. In groups of about 6-8 persons, read Mark 10:45 and Philippians 2:5-11. Discuss these questions: In what ways is the concept of humble service an appropriate umbrella concept for the character of Christ as the measure of maturity? What values for your children can you identify as growing out of this concept of humble service? In what ways can you recognize and cultivate these values in your children? The groups do not need to report to each other.

5. Divide into 3 groups. Group 1 will examine Galatians 5:22-23, group 2 Romans 12:9-12, and group 3 Matthew 5:3-12. Each group is to draw on its assigned Scripture passage as the raw data for writing a definition of the mature character of Christ. (*Note:* You may have used a similar activity in session 2. If so, refer back to the definitions the group arrived at then. The Romans passage was not mentioned at that point, so you may want to focus on it.) They should write these definitions on newsprint sheets to be read to the entire group. Discuss together the similarities and differences of these definitions. In what ways can these Scripture passages guide you as parents in shaping the values of your children? If your group would like to spend an extra session, perhaps as an evening together in someone's home, repeat this exercise with the entire Sermon on the Mount (Matt. 5-7).

6. Review your personal maturity assessment on page 88. Discuss with your group the effects your own state of maturity has on the development of your children's value systems. In what ways can you help your children by attending to your own maturity issues?

7. Form groups of 3 or 4 people with spouses in different groups. Look back over your assessment of the maturity of each of your children on page 89. In these groups, share with each other one specific step you can take with each of your children this week to address a need in their current process of maturity development. Plan to share the results with each other at the beginning of next week's session. If you have time, you may pray for each other in your group time. In any case, make a point to pray for your partners throughout the week.

Closing

Take a few moments of individual, quiet meditation to read Psalm 78:1-8. Make note of the psalmist's relationships with past and future generations. Write a brief prayer reflecting your feelings about these same relationships. Those who wish to may read their prayers for the group before dismissing.

---

[1]Yancey, Philip. "How Your Faith Affects Your Teenagers." *Moody Monthly*, December 1975, p. 57. Chicago: Moody Press.
[2]Ward, Ted. *The Influence of Secular Institutions on Today's Family*, pp. 10, 11.

SIX

THE CONVERSATIONS CONTINUE

This chapter is different from the previous five. In place of narrative and explanation it offers conversations. If you read and think about these conversation scripts carefully, you may find that they help you integrate what you have been learning about authority with your real family relationships.

So take some time to read through the conversations below and talk about them with your spouse, with older children, and with others in your study group. Consider the ways in which the people in the script are similar to and different from your own families. If you are part of a study group, you may find it interesting to reread the scripts in your group session. Invite group members to volunteer for the roles in the script and read the conversation aloud to each other. Reading with feeling and identification with the characters will increase the value of this session.

Part 1 of the script is a conversation between four couples discussing parental authority as it relates to their children. Part 2 is a conversation between five teenagers. In both cases the conversations are real, and were transcribed with the cooperation of the participants. They have been condensed, and details have been altered to preserve confidentiality.

Questions for stimulating thought and group discussion follow the script. Since not all questions will fit every situation, select the most appropriate questions for your group.

Part 1: Parents

In this script, eight parents talk about the authority issues that trouble them the most as they deal with their children. Four of the parents have teenage children. The other four have younger families. The script was drawn from a whole evening of conversation between the eight.

Father 1:

We had just moved into a new neighborhood and had let our son Philip go over to the swimming pool. He was supposed to be home at a set time, and he didn't make it by a long shot.

Mother 1:

He was three hours late.

Father 1:

We knew where he was, but we just gave him the rope to let him hang himself—which he did. And, even though it was summer vacation, we followed with two weeks worth of "You're in your room." He spent the time stripping the walls and getting them ready to be painted.

Like I said, this all happened shortly after we moved in, and we discovered later that our use of this kind of discipline affected our entire neighborhood. The kids were mad at us and our son because other parents saw that we could get away with keeping Philip in his room for two solid weeks.

Mother 1:

It was hot up there. It was a very hot summer.

Father 1:

We haven't had too much trouble with him since, and the other two are time conscious too—probably because of what happened to Philip. Now, perhaps we went a little overboard, and I often wonder if we did. But we *did* accomplish what we wanted for him—and in just one experience.

Mother 1:

I don't think Philip knew what the punishment was going to be beforehand. But I don't know if that really makes any difference. What it comes down to is that he was testing out a new situation, and he discovered the consequences for not following the rules.

Father 2:

One thing that we ran into recently was a problem with the car. Alan drives the Dodge, and we live on a narrow street. It was winter, and the streets were slippery and snowy, so Jean had asked him to move his car into the driveway.

Mother 2:

He meant to ask his brother to move it in before he went to bed, but he forgot.

Father 2:

The next morning when he went out to go to school, the driver's side door was smashed in. His punishment was that he had to take care of the repair. We told him, "O.K., Alan, we told you what to do, and you didn't do it, and now you'll suffer the consequences. It's your repair bill." So his forgetfulness cost him $350.

Mother 2:

Alan didn't make a whole lot of fuss over having to pay, and I think we did the right thing by letting him pay for the repair.

Father 3:

Our son is only three, so we don't run into quite the same problems as you do. Every day Jeff is into something new. He's not necessarily being bad—he's just exploring because he's full of energy and life. It's just very hard for either of us to keep track of what he's up to.

Mother 4:

I think I know what you mean. Jonathan is about that age too. I think he's going through a transition period.

Father 4:

Mom and Dad are going through a transition period. Especially since the baby came.

Mother 4:

There are times when things go well, and I don't have to get after him a lot. One thing I am happy for is that we read with him, and he has an interest in books. I'm not sure that has anything to do with discipline, though.

Father 4:

The times when he is challenging are hard on me, I guess. Maybe that's why they don't go so well. If he doesn't obey, I just take away whatever it is he has. Like last night, I asked him not to shine the flashlight in my face. He forgot, and I took the light away. So right now that's how I deal with things: by taking things away when he doesn't listen. It's hard though.

Mother 4:

And it doesn't seem to make the problem go away. He just grabs something else . . .

Mother 2:

I remember another time when we had to make our rules about the car stick. For some reason we had two cars on a business vacation a while ago. Alan wanted to drive back nonstop while we dropped a friend off in a town on the way.

Father 2:

On that one I just said, "No, you're going to stop with us." Alan started to say something, and I said, "No discussion." I felt I was right and explained why. It's just a safety factor. If two vehicles are traveling together and one has trouble, the other can stop and help. Even adults would do that. I think my explanation helped him see the safety factors involved; he just hadn't thought of them before.

Mother 2:

I think our kids feel we have been fair with them because they usually don't get upset and pout when we tell them, "This is the way it is." Alan teases his father now. He'll just look at him and say, "No discussion."

Mother 1:

Our kids almost always respond when we "lay down the law." I don't worry about them responding. But sometimes their criticisms make me uncertain whether I'm doing the right thing.

Mother 3:

It seems like I feel most secure about authority when I'm alone with my family. My expectations of my children are a little easier to lay down. If I have to exert my authority in front of some other parent, I feel kind of insecure. I wonder if he or she is thinking I'm a little too stern or too easygoing.

Father 1:

I was thinking I feel more secure when I'm *out* of my own situation, because I think I handle it better than I do at home. I don't blow my stack, and I react more positively in front of other people than I do at home. I guess I'm more aware of what I'm doing when I know other people are watching. So I do what I'm supposed to do in public, but at home I don't.

Father 2:

In the past I felt insecure about exerting my authority in the area of the "do's and don'ts" recommended by the church we used to belong to—rules like, "Don't go to the movies" and that type of thing. I felt I ought to back up their standards and exert some kind of authority, but I didn't really believe that stuff myself. Now my wife and I have come up with our own standards—ones we feel comfortable with and feel right about enforcing. That makes it a lot easier to be consistent.

Mother 3:

Sometimes I wonder if our decisions aren't arbitrary—especially on matters like what time the child has to go to bed. We've been through that a lot lately—a lot of arguments about which child goes to bed in which time frame. It's obvious that if they don't get the proper sleep, they'll be cranky the next day. But they still argue, "Jimmy down the street gets to stay up till midnight."

Father 1:

Something we have talked about before that kind of relates to the bedtime issue is trying to let the child gradually break away from our standards and start making his or her own decisions. I don't know if we're allowing enough freedom in this area. Sometimes when Philip questions my decisions, I will ask him what he would have done. Often he comes up with solutions that are perfectly valid and would work as well as mine—sometimes better. That's a little hard for me to accept, even though I know that he's already thirteen years old and a real thinker.

Father 4:

I was just thinking that when children are very young, they learn exactly how much they can get away with. It starts when they are a year or two old and continues forever. I'm sure by the time Jonathan is ten or twelve it will be too late to start saying, "Now you're going to start minding me."

Mother 4:

Well, I think my inconsistency has caused Jonathan to react the way he does at his age. The problem is not so much changing him as changing myself.

Father 2:

What strikes me about inconsistency is that my children learn to be inconsistent in the same ways I am. For example, I really don't want my son to lose his temper, and I was just telling people how important that is to me last night. But I think if you polled our family, you would find that *I'm* the one with the short fuse. I sure blew it yesterday. That dog of ours got to me, I'm afraid. He had gotten off the rope and was running all over the park. So I tied him up with tight knots. A while later I came to check on the dog, and the rope had been cut through the knots. I was not controlling myself very well, and when I found David, I told him that was a very stupid thing to do. Then he told me why he had done it. At his mother's direction, David had come to get the dog and couldn't get the knots untied, so he cut them with his pocket knife. I don't know why I reacted that way. I was really upset over that whole situation, and I can't put my finger on why I was so upset.

Father 1:

I find it particularly difficult being left alone with the children. I'm out of the house like most working fathers—maybe a little more since I travel. But on Saturday, Alice was out shopping and running errands. One of the boys came in and asked if he could go someplace. The trouble is, I don't know what the limits are. I don't know that they can go to the park but they can't go to so-and-so's house. So I often come back with, "Does your mother let you do that?" or "Would your mother approve if she were here?"

For me that's the approach that makes the best sense. I'm not really afraid they are trying to hoodwink me, but they may be trying to do something that they normally couldn't do. They're saying, "Mom's not here; we'll see what Dad will allow." Not that I think they would do something really wrong. They're usually pretty good.

Mother 4:

I think the hardest time is when I know Jonathan is challenging me. Or when he's doing something knowing that I'm going to react and get upset. I know he's doing it just to get the negative reaction from me, and it's awfully hard for me to switch it around to a positive reaction. He's in a stage now where he just goes around and drops his toys everywhere. Right now our apartment is a disaster, and it's not because it hasn't been cleaned in a month. I pick up several times every day. He does play with the toys a little; he's not just dumping them. But he leaves them scattered everywhere. At times it's really obvious that he's just trying to get my goat. That's what's hardest—when I think he knows that he's doing something just to provoke me.

Part 2: Teens

In part 1, parents talked about how they used their authority in relationship to their children. Any relationship that involves either authority or conflict, as parent-child relationships do, has two sides. Now you will have a chance to hear how a group of teens perceive their parents' authority and discipline.

None of these teens are children of any of the parents in part 1. However, they are all children of Christian parents, and the script was drawn from an hour's church discussion group. In spite of some of the questioning and hostility that is evident, these young people cooperated in the discussion with the hope of helping parents and children to build better relationships. Some even said they hoped it might be valuable to them and their parents. So pay attention as they begin by talking about the strategies their parents use to get them to do things they don't want to do.

Boy 1:

My parents try to make me feel guilty if I don't do what they want.

Boy 2:

Yeah, they say, "If you love me, you'll do this for me."

Girl 1:

They make you feel like if you don't do it, you don't love them.

Boy 2:

Or they bring up things like, "We've done so much for you. We brought you up since you were a little kid."

Boy 1:

And when we have a conflict—you know, disagree about something—they always win.

Boy 2:

No, they don't always win.

Boy 1:

They might win, but a lot of times they end up giving in anyway.

Boy 3:

Yeah, after you get the point across that it's their fault or something.

Boy 1:

Fight them long enough and they'll say, "Oh, I'm sick of fighting—go ahead and do it."

Boy 2:

They make you feel so guilty.

Boy 1:

They win somehow. They either make you feel guilty, or they prove you're totally wrong.

Boy 3:

Sometimes they go back to their time and say, "When we were fifteen years old, we didn't do this and this."

Boy 2:

"We did everything for our parents."

Girl 2:

"I had to clean the whole house and make all the beds and didn't get an allowance. We did things out of love."

Boy 2:

Grounding . . .

All others:
Oh, grounding!

Boy 2:
Grounding is so dumb. It doesn't do anything for me.

Girl 2:
I think it's kind of an incentive for the kid—especially if you really like hanging around with other people. It's kind of a hassle being grounded because you don't get to do anything but sit inside and watch TV or whatever.

Boy 3:
I get the car taken away.

Girl 1:
So do I.

Boy 3:
I can't live without an automobile.

Boy 2:
I guess sometimes you learn something from punishments like that—even though you don't recognize it at the time.

Boy 1:
But a lot of times it makes you even more mad and more rebellious.

Girl 2:
It just creates resentment. It's so easy to get a hassle started. They tell you to do something, and you don't want to do it, so you start complaining. It's much smarter to tell them you're going to do something, because then they sometimes start it for you.

Girl 1:
My Dad doesn't ask, he implies. That makes me so mad. He'll talk to someone else. Like, he'll say, "June, why doesn't Sharon help you?" Or he'll be talking to the dog and say, "Freckles, you want Sharon to take you for a walk?" I'm sitting right there—come on!

Boy 3:
Someone want to take the dog for a walk? (laughter)

Girl 1:
Sometimes to get him, I'll say, "Hey Mom, you want Dad to help you?"

Boy 1:
They don't go about it in a direct way. They always take a side road.

Boy 3:

Because if they go straight to the question, they know they're going to get friction.

Girl 2:

I find that parents are sometimes impatient. Yesterday I was doing my homework. I was doing French, and you have to concentrate on the verb tense. My mother called out a couple of times, and I kept answering, "Yes, just a minute. Let me finish this one verb." But she came up and pulled me downstairs.

Boy 2:

You don't get to finish your thing. You have to do their thing right away.

Girl 1:

A lot of times when they do that, they're just trying to exercise their power and authority over you. "I'm your parent, and you're going to do what I say."

Girl 2:

When I ask for an explanation, it's always, "Because I said so."

Boy 3:

Parents don't have to have a reason to do the things they do.

Boy 1:

"Because I'm your father or mother . . . "

Boy 2:

What kind of reason is that?

Girl 1:

When you ask what they're going to do, they say, "You don't have to know." When I want to go out, my Dad will ask me all these questions. But when he leaves and I ask him when he'll be back, he says, "You don't have to know that."

Boy 2:

It's a double standard. My parents will tell me not to do something, and then they'll slip and do it. Then I say, "You yell at me for doing it. Why are you doing it?" And they say, "Oh, because I'm older than you."

Boy 3:

"Just wait until you're a parent."

Girl 1:

Sometimes they'll be yelling at me about something I did, and I say, "Well, you've done that sometimes." They say, "We're not talking about *us* right now—we're talking about *you.*"

Other times I'll tell them that they did something and they'll say, "Well, you did it too." I'll say, "We're not talking about *me*—we're talking about *you.*" Then they get mad.

Boy 2:

And they won't say they were wrong. They'll say they're sorry for yelling or something like that. But they won't say what they were yelling about was wrong. They just say, "I'm sorry I lost my temper."

Boy 1:

They can never let you win. If you do, you lose anyway because you feel guilty.

Boy 2:

They say, "Oh, go ahead and do it, I don't care," but they're thinking, "Ha! Ha! You'll never do it without feeling guilty."

Girl 2:

I don't feel that way. I think that sometimes parents don't insist on winning. Sometimes when I get into an argument with my mother, she says, "Your girlfriend always does her housework, but you never seem to do anything around here." I don't know what to say to that, so I just stand there and take it all. But then she comes back to me later and says, "I apologize for what I said. You *do* help a lot around here. I just must have been in a bad mood." I really appreciate it when she does that.

Boy 1:

I find ways of manipulating my parents—sometimes by being nice. Often the best way to get what I want is not to argue but to kind of play along.

Boy 2:

Sometimes I think that whether you win or not is not the point. Basically, what's important is whether you reach an agreement between the two of you—not necessarily a compromise but at least an understanding. If you can come to an understanding between you and your parents, maybe they'll realize something that they've been doing wrong and apologize for it and try to make it right, and you'll do the same. I've had that happen once or twice.

Girl 2:

Well, my parents don't really have that many rules set down. Or maybe they do, and I just follow them automatically. Like, I know that I have to be in at 10:30 at the latest. They never told me to be in at 10:30. I just think 10:30 is the latest. I mean, I'll never get up for school the next morning if I go to bed too late. I automatically tell them where I'm going and who I'm with too. I do my chores and all that, and they never have to tell me to clean my room, because my room is always clean.

Girl 1:

Well, I have to clean my room every week. What I hate is my mother makes a list on paper of what I have to do, and I already *know* what I have to do, so that really really bugs me. She does it on purpose because she knows . . .

Boy 2:

She writes it in red in big bold letters, "Clean your room; vacuum the steps; clean the basement."

Girl 1:

I *know* what to do, and yet she does it just to bug me. But they trust me with some other big things. Like the car. I think for me it's a pretty big deal for them to let me use the car as much as I do. After I had that accident and everything, I thought they might only let me drive once a week, if at all.

Boy 3:

It depends on whether you're going with Joe Freak or Joe Goody whether they let you have the car or stay out late.

Boy 2:

My parents show a definite lack of trust when it comes to the car. They say when you're old enough to buy a car, that's when you're old enough to drive and have responsibility. That's weird, because I can buy a car now, and they still won't let me.

Girl 2:

I think my parents trust me with the way I handle my money. They used to always take it away and not let me do anything with it.

Girl 1:

Is this money you get by working?

Girl 2:

Yes.

Girl 1:

I don't understand that. Why do parents have rights to your money?

Boy 3:

Why do parents have rights to anything about you?

Boy 2:

They did everything for you. I mean, they raised you from a little infant.

Girl 1:

They consider you theirs.

Boy 1:

They spend so much money on you every year.

Girl 2:

You won't ever be able to pay your parents back for what they spent on you.

Girl 1:

You've got to pay them back? You're paying them back by loving them and becoming something. Maybe even by being something like them.

Boy 2:

I guess you might even do some of the things they do that bug you now. I hope I can improve on some of the things about my parents I don't like. I mean, I've often thought, "I'll never do this when I'm a parent," but who knows how much of that I'll remember?

Girl 2:

I think most kids look up to their parents and take them as an example.

Suggestions for Group Session

Opening

Get back together with the group of three or four people you met with in session 5. Review the steps you wanted to take with your children this past week, and compare notes on what happened. Encourage each other and pray together for your children.

In these groups, read Matthew 21:28-32. Discuss the ways in which the dilemma of this father reflects the struggles you experience in using your authority to serve your children. Pray for insight as you draw this study to a conclusion.

For Discussion

Questions for Part 1: Parents

1. Do you feel the father whose son was late returning from swimming was fair when he said, "We just gave him the rope to let him hang himself?" Relate this to the principles of problem ownership, trust, and building responsibility.

2. Evaluate the punishment of "two weeks worth of 'You're in your room'" in light of the father's wondering if they "went a little overboard."

3. What do you think these parents were trying to accomplish? How well do you think they did at achieving their goals?

4. What implications do you see in the mother's comment that she didn't think that her son knew in advance what the punishment would be in that situation?

5. Whose responsibility do you think the smashed car door is? Why?

6. How do you feel about making Alan pay the bill and his passive response to it?

7. How would you distinguish between energetic curiosity and being bad?

8. Who do you think goes through more transition periods: parents or children? Why?

9. Jonathan's mother says she is not sure that the reason he enjoys books has anything to do with discipline. What do you think?

10. Jonathan's parents seem to sense that taking things away from him is counterproductive. What would you suggest as an alternative?

11. When Alan wanted to drive back home alone and his father said, "no," and "no discussion," do you think he really meant no discussion? In what situations might parents be wisest to say "no discussion allowed on this topic"?

12. This group of parents discusses where they feel more secure in their authority: at home or in public. Which is easiest for you and why?

13. How would you help the father who felt he should use his authority to back up the church's standards, even though he didn't agree with them? How do you feel about his solution to the problem?

14. How can you distinguish between a parental decision that is genuinely in the child's best interests and one that is arbitrary, or only in the parents' interest?

15. The father of thirteen-year-old Philip has a hard time accepting that his son has much wisdom to contribute. What would you suggest this father do to encourage his son's participation in problem-solving?

16. Evaluate the importance of the preschool years against the teen years in establishing patterns. Is it ever too late to change?

17. React to Jonathan's mother's statement that the problem is not so much changing him as changing herself.

18. Inconsistency is almost a universal bugaboo of parents. What remedy would you suggest?

19. The father in the dog-and-rope episode says, "I can't put my finger on why I was so upset." What ideas do you have?

20. What do you think of the father who does not always know the standards his wife sets for his children, and so has a problem enforcing them when she's not around? How can you help him out of this dilemma?

21. How can you tell when a child is doing something just to provoke you? What kind of response is best in these situations?

Questions for Part 2—Teens

1. These teens mention guilt feelings repeatedly. Identify the sources of these feelings. Do you think their parents are really trying to stimulate guilt feelings? What do you think the parents might be able to do about this? Do you think guilt feelings are good motivators to desired behavior?

2. Respond to the statement by the boy who said, "They win somehow. They either make you feel guilty or they prove you're totally wrong."

3. Grounding seems to be an almost universal punishment. However, the teens didn't like it and were divided as to whether it worked. Evaluate the meaning and effectiveness of grounding. What creative alternatives could you propose?

4. The teens didn't like their parents comparing what things were like for their generation to the current situation. Why do you think parents use this technique? What could help them break the habit?

5. One of the boys says, "I guess sometimes you learn something from punishments like that—even though you don't recognize it at the time." In what ways could parents help their children learn more from the difficulties they face together?

6. One of the girls says, "My Dad doesn't ask, he implies. He'll talk to someone else." What do you suppose makes parents reluctant to

speak directly to their children? What are the results of this sideways communication? How can the situation be corrected?

7. The teens complained about a number of situations in which they sense a double standard. Their parents' expectations of them are higher than their expectations of themselves. Identify situations in which this may be true. Do you think that parents' position of authority entitles them to this sort of privilege?

8. The teens also complained that their parents do things just to assert their authority. How do you feel about some of the expressions they mentioned: "I'm your parent, and you're going to do what I say." "Because I said so." "Because I'm your father or mother." "Just wait until you're a parent"?

9. Whether or not they ever use them on their parents, these teens have come up with a number of clever responses to their parents. Their parents' response to these "techniques" might be, "Don't get smart." To what extent do you think the teens are just "being smart" and to what extent are they trying to establish what they see as justice? What more effective strategy could you suggest for parents in these situations?

10. These teens perceive their parents' apologies as dealing with form rather than substance. "They will say they were sorry for yelling or something like that. They won't say what they were yelling about was wrong." Under what conditions do you think a parent owes a child an apology?

11. The teens admit to manipulating their parents. What can parents do to be on guard against manipulation and keep communication honest and straightforward?

12. The response to rules varies from compliance with unexpressed expectations to rebellion at what seem to be insulting demands. What kinds of rules really help the family and what kinds are barriers to communication?

13. Despite all the negatives, these teens perceive that their parents trust them. Money and cars are mentioned, though a couple of reservations are added in. In what ways can parents show their trust in their children?

14. The teens seem to have a sense of "paying back" what their parents have invested in time and money. How do you feel about this attitude?

15. What do you think are the chances that these teens will improve on the jobs their parents have done with them?

Closing

Read how the father of the prodigal son treats him in Luke 15:11-32. In what ways is he a grace-oriented parent? How does he use his authority to serve both of his sons?

As you conclude this time together, discuss with each other what you have learned through this course. Focus on the benefits you have received by completing sentences such as these:

"I learned that I . . ."

"I discovered that I . . ."

"I am glad that I . . ."

"I want to change that I . . ."

Finish with a prayer time, thanking God for what you have learned from each other and asking for God's wisdom and strength to serve your children as God's agents of authority in their lives.